MAN

TO

MAN

MAN TO MAN

BECOMING THE BELIEVER GOD CALLED YOU TO BE

DENNIS E. HENSLEY

Man to Man: Becoming the Believer God Called You to Be

© 2003 by Dennis E. Hensley

Published by Kregel Publications, a division of Kregel, Inc., P.O. Box 2607, Grand Rapids, MI 49501.

Unless otherwise indicated, Scripture quotations are from the King James Version of the Holy Bible.

Scripture quotations marked NIV are from the *Holy Bible, New International Version®*. NIV®. © 1973, 1978, 1984 by International Bible Society. Used by permission of Zondervan Publishing House. All rights reserved.

Scripture quotations marked NASB are from the *New American Standard Bible*. © The Lockman Foundation 1960, 1962, 1963, 1968, 1971, 1972, 1973, 1975, 1977, 1995. Used by permission.

Cover design: John M. Lucas

Library of Congress Cataloging-in-Publication Data
Hensley, Dennis E.
Man to man: becoming the believer God called you to be /
by Dennis E. Hensley.
    p. cm.
Includes bibliographical references.
    1. Men—Prayer books and devotions—English. 2.
Men—Religious life. I. Title.
BV4843.H39   2003
242'.642—dc22   2003015984

ISBN 0-8254-2791-6

Printed in the United States of America

03 04 05 06 07 / 5 4 3 2 1

This book is fondly dedicated to
Daryl R. Yost, Ed.D.,
retired Vice President of Taylor University.

His gracious Christian spirit, his tireless energy
on behalf of students and colleagues, his ability
to take a personal interest in the goals and dreams of
others, and his moral walk as an administrator, educator,
husband, father, and grandfather have made him
a role model for me.

Contents

Preface 9
Acknowledgments 11

Chapter 1:   The Missing Ingredient in Prayer 13
Chapter 2:   Hard Work Is Still in Vogue 19
Chapter 3:   Spiritual Hypoxia 25
Chapter 4:   Rescue the Perishing 31
Chapter 5:   Recycling Righteous Rubbish 37
Chapter 6:   Making Christian Service a Joy 43
Chapter 7:   Prayers for the Sick: Why They Are and
              Sometimes *Aren't* Answered 49
Chapter 8:   I Can Read You Like a Book 57
Chapter 9:   The Prepaid Debt 63
Chapter 10:   The House of God 69
Chapter 11:   Drifting Without Direction 75
Chapter 12:   The Scent of Death 81
Chapter 13:   Waving from the Shores 87
Chapter 14:   The Voice of God 91
Chapter 15:   The Original "Blood, Sweat, and Tears"
              Speech 97

Chapter 16: What's Cooking? 103
Chapter 17: It's Always New Year's Eve for a Christian 107
Chapter 18: Godly Gumption Overcomes Shyness 113
Chapter 19: Get Up and Grow 119
Chapter 20: An Instant of Understanding 125
Chapter 21: You Are What You Eat 131
Chapter 22: Tracing Your Spiritual Genealogy 137
Chapter 23: Too Obvious to Accept As Truth 143
Chapter 24: If Life's a Jungle, Become a Trailblazer 151
Chapter 25: The Apostle John's "Ten Must Wanted" List ... 157
Chapter 26: A Penny for Your Thoughts About America ... 163
Chapter 27: Dropping a Biblical Plumb Line 169
Chapter 28: The Revealing Light 175
Chapter 29: Whom Do You Trust? 179
Chapter 30: The Regenerating Remnant 185
Chapter 31: The X Factor in Christmas 191

PREFACE

Because this book provides men with views of various aspects of the Christian life, it can be used in a variety of ways.

It can be read for a month as daily *personal devotions.* Each of the thirty-one chapters can be finished in about fifteen minutes, yet each provides a topic for deeper thought, further consideration, and personal contemplation. The topics are particularly focused on the challenges facing twenty-first-century Christian men in their roles as leaders in their homes, communities, churches, and businesses.

The book can also be used as an aid in *one-on-one mentoring.* Any mature Christian man who is nurturing a recent convert or is guiding the spiritual growth of a younger man will find that this book will assist in that nurturing process. Each chapter takes biblical stories and lines of Scripture and shows how they apply to contemporary life. Many of the questions raised by new believers are given simple, pragmatic responses within these pages.

This book can serve as a *tool for witnessing.* Its use of anecdotes, humor, human interest stories, and sound advice make it very "readable," even from a secular viewpoint. The gospel message is clear throughout the book, but it is presented in a nonthreatening, nonoverbearing way. This book can be loaned to a friend, coworker, business acquaintance, customer, or any other man who likes to learn something while also enjoying a good story.

Additionally, this book would serve well as a discussion starter for *men's prayer groups* or *men's home Bible study meetings.* Each chapter draws attention to needs in our daily lives: matters that can be expanded on through discussion or question-and-answer sessions.

ACKNOWLEDGMENTS

I wish to offer public thanks to specific people who have nurtured me as a writer, a teacher, and an ever-evolving Christian: my parents, Ed and Juanita Hensley; my siblings, Gary and Pam Hensley; my wife and children, Rose, Nathan, and Jeanette; my Taylor University colleagues Doug Barcalow, Ron Sloan, Pam Jordan, Bud Hamilton, and Dwight Jessup; my devoted editor friends Joan Guest, Steve Laube, Janyre Tromp, Joan Alexander, Lin Johnson, Steve Barclift, Marlene Chase, Reg Forder, and Jack Williams; and my longtime fellow wordsmiths Jim Riordan, Bill Myers, John Ingrisano, Michael Smith, Jerry Jenkins, Les Stobbe, and Ken Wales.

CHAPTER 1

THE MISSING INGREDIENT
IN PRAYER

Not long ago a man said to me, "I'd pray more if I believed it would do any good."

I responded, "You've got the cause and effect reversed. The fact is, you'd believe more if you would pray more."

Like this man, other men have come to me for counseling because they were despondent over the fact that God had not answered their prayers. As ridiculous as it may seem, after talking with them I've discovered that many of these men never made their needs known to God in the first place. They assumed "there was no need to pray since God already knows the needs."

Indeed, God knows every need; but we were created for fellowship with Him and prayer is an important aspect of that fellowship. David understood this. He pledged, "Unto thee will I pray" (Ps. 5:2); "evening, and morning, and at noon, will I pray" (55:17).

Daniel prayed three times each day even though it meant risking his life to do so. Solomon dropped to his knees in submission and prayed a dedication prayer after the building of the temple. John the Baptist spent a lifetime of fasting, praying, and preaching in the wilderness.

No one would deny that these men were close to God. Nevertheless, they were unassuming and humble. They poured out their feelings and thoughts to God through prayer and earnestly sought His guidance in all matters. Their conviction that their God was a caring, listening God prompted them to turn to Him with an intensity of prayer. They prayed believing that God would respond.

I heard a preacher once explain the basis of prayer power. He said, "It's not the length of your prayers—how long they are; it's not the arithmetic of your prayers—how many there are; it's not the poetry of your prayers—how beautiful they are; it's not the volume of your prayers—how loud they are. It's the intensity. That's all that counts."

If we look for the ultimate example of prayer intensity, we will find it in the prayers of Jesus. He preceded all of His miracles—from the feeding of the five thousand to the raising of Lazarus from the dead—with intense prayer. Nowhere is this better depicted than in Luke 22:41 and 44, when Jesus prayed that His human flesh would be strong enough to face and endure the crucifixion before Him:

> And he was withdrawn from them about a stone's cast, and kneeled down, and prayed, ... and being in an agony he prayed more earnestly: and his sweat was as it were great drops of blood falling down to the ground.

Such earnest prayers cannot go unanswered from a loving God. In that instance, Jesus was given the strength He requested: "And there appeared an angel unto him from heaven, strengthening him" (Luke 22:43).

It is important to note two important things about the example of prayer Jesus set for us in the garden. First, there is the fact that He made a personal request. He asked to be spared the pending death on the cross. In asking this, however, He qualified His request by saying that it should be denied if it was not in line with the will of God the Father. He yielded His will to the Father's.

When it was apparent that such a request could not be granted, the second thing Jesus prayed for was the strength *to do* the Father's will.

This request was granted. God has a plan for our lives that we are free to reject or submit to. Following God's leading brings us our greatest fulfillment, although yielding is seldom easy.

The power of prayer is God empowering us to do what is right in His eyes. Thus, we must emulate Jesus in this way: by making our needs and desires known to God, but to ask that they be granted only if they are pleasing to Him and along the calling He has for us.

I can personally vouch for the fact that yielding to God is difficult if it means accepting something other than that for which you have been praying. In 1974 I suffered damage to the nerves near my left temple. The result was gross disfigurement of the entire left side of my face. My cheek sagged, my left eyelid would not blink, my lips were twisted, half of my tongue was numb, and my forehead would not wrinkle on the left side. It was terrifying.

Instinctively, my prayers were for a miraculous total recovery. I prayed fervently, but no healing came. After ten days in our city hospital, I was transferred to a large university research hospital. While there, a young hospital chaplain stopped by for a visit. I told him I had prayed for my face to be healed but there had been no improvement.

The chaplain opened his Bible and spent time reading me the Old Testament story of how Joseph was sold into slavery by his jealous brothers. By the story's end, Joseph had become the second most powerful man in Egypt. When he revealed his identity to his brothers, they were sure he would seek revenge. Instead, he forgave them. When they asked how he could be so magnanimous, he explained that God had used their evil to work His good.

"Now, you have a similar opportunity," the chaplain told me. "Life has dealt you a hard blow. Is your faith strong enough for you to stop praying for what *you* want and, instead, discover what good God can bring out of this?"

"But I'm paralyzed," I mumbled through twisted and numb lips.

"Just the one side of your face is," the chaplain countered. "Your legs, feet, hands, arms, and back work fine. So does your hearing, thinking, seeing, and sense of touch. Find out what God has in store for you. Yield to Him."

From then on I changed my prayer. I continued to ask for my face to be healed, but I also prayed that if that was not part of God's will for me, then I wished for the grace to accept my situation and to serve where He could use me.

To my total amazement, the paralysis turned out to be a complete blessing from God. I had to attend speech therapy class in order to learn how to speak clearly again. I was given tips on vocal projection, enunciation, delivery, and body language. Soon, I not only learned how to speak again, I developed into a public orator. Thanks to that training years ago, I now deliver more than eighty major speeches each year at colleges, universities, and corporations. I also teach a Sunday school class each week and make numerous guest appearances on radio and television stations. Had it not been for the paralysis, this phase of my career might never have opened itself to me.

In the years since 1974 I have regained the feeling and most of the motor movement of my forehead, nose, lips, and tongue. My eyelids and left cheek still show evidences of the original nerve damage, however. But I never think about it. If people ever ask me about it, I tell them, "It was something that seemed to start out bad, but through the power of prayer it wound up working to my good."

So, if you ever catch yourself saying, "I'd pray more if I thought it would do me any good," just change that to, "I'm praying *now*, Lord, so that I can discover what *is good* for my life!"

THINKING MORE ABOUT CHAPTER 1

Scripture Verses to Ponder

O thou that hearest prayer, unto thee shall all flesh come.
—Psalm 65:2

I give myself unto prayer.
—Psalm 109:4

The sacrifice of the wicked is an abomination to the LORD: but the prayer of the upright is his delight.

—Proverbs 15:8

And all things, whatsoever ye shall ask in prayer, believing, ye shall receive.

—Matthew 21:22

But we will give ourselves continually to prayer, and to the ministry of the word.

—Acts 6:4

Be careful for nothing; but in every thing by prayer and supplication with thanksgiving let your requests be made known unto God. And the peace of God, which passeth all understanding, shall keep your hearts and minds through Christ Jesus.

—Philippians 4:6–7

Questions to Consider

1. Jesus often prayed, both alone and with His disciples. What instances can you recall when Jesus prayed? What was the focus of His prayers? What were the intents of His prayers? What were the results of His prayers? What lessons can you learn from this to apply to your own prayer life?

2. In chapter 7 we will discuss in more detail the reasons why prayers sometimes are and other times are not answered. For now, however, spend a moment recalling a time when you thought your prayers weren't being answered. Can you think of a reason *why* the prayers were not answered? Have the prayers since been answered? With the perspective of time, can you see the hand of God at work in the way your prayers were or were not responded to?

3. Are your prayers often generic, nonspecific, and routine? If so, take a moment to list a half-dozen genuine things you feel you should be concentrating on in your prayers. After making the list, keep it handy and use it to guide your prayers for the next week.

   A.

   B.

   C.

   D.

   E.

   F.

4. Has anyone ever supported you during a crisis by praying for you? Why not call that person today to say thanks for that love?

SUGGESTED ADDITIONAL READINGS

Blanchard, Charles A. *Getting Things from God.* Wheaton, Ill.: Victor Books, 1985.

Clark, Gordon. *Revelation and the Bible.* Grand Rapids: Baker, 1958.

Hensley, Dennis E. *How to Fulfill Your Potential: Physical, Emotional, and Spiritual Harmony.* Anderson: Warner Press, 1989.

Pentecost, J. Dwight. *The Words and Works of Jesus Christ.* Grand Rapids: Zondervan, 1981.

Ryle, J. C. *Holiness.* London: Hunt, 1899.

CHAPTER 2

HARD WORK IS
STILL IN VOGUE

Christian men who run into difficulty in the business area of their lives often come to me for advice and counseling. I'm always glad to offer suggestions and ideas if I feel I can help these men out of their difficulties. Unfortunately, all too often, people wait to ask my advice until long after they are head over heels in financial disaster or are already headed for a meeting with the IRS. Such was the case of one man I know.

A few years ago a fellow who attended my church decided to start his own business. His job at the time required that he work out of state as a traveling "troubleshooter" for a network of corporate computers. This enabled the man to see his family just two weekends out of each month. He felt that this was not a proper way to serve as the head of his family, so on an impulse he took quick and drastic steps to alter his lifestyle. He quit his job and announced that he was moving home and going into business for himself. He withdrew all of the savings he and his wife had put into the bank over a fourteen-year period and used this as seed money for his new enterprise.

At first things seemed to be just as he had imagined. He was able to spend more time with his wife and children, didn't have to travel from state to state anymore, and could sit all day in his home office designing new computer programs (his greatest joy). Ah, the life of a self-employed entrepreneur. How sweet it seemed to be.

Six months later, however, my friend had exhausted all of his financial reserves and he was starting to fall behind with his debts. True, his computer consulting firm was starting to get a foothold, but to date he had secured only seven steady clients, and none of those seven was a big-paying operation. The man came to me in desperation.

"The Lord just doesn't seem to be blessing me," he said with a heartsick moan. "I thought I was doing the right thing by coming home to be with my family. I expected God to provide opportunities for me, to open doors, to help my business prosper. He hasn't done that. I want to know why."

As we continued to talk, the man admitted to me that the main reason he went into the computer consulting business was because he enjoyed working on the machinery and designing new programs. What he hated, however, was sales work. As such, during the first six months of his business he had mailed out four thousand advertising brochures, but he had not made even one phone call or personal visit to potential clients. He expected the brochures and "God's blessing" to generate big profits for him.

I opened my Bible and read Genesis 3:19 to him: "By the sweat of your brow you will eat your food" (NIV). I then turned to the New Testament and read the story of the sower, found in Matthew 13:3–8.

"Rewards must be earned," I summarized. "The Bible promises no free lunch. God expects each of us to subdue the earth in whatever career we've chosen. That may mean working extra hours, learning new skills, or accepting new challenges."

"But I've mailed out brochures," he protested.

"And they've drawn seven clients to you," I responded. "That's good. But now you need to try other things. When the sower went out to sow, he threw seed *everywhere.* The birds ate some, the weeds killed some, the sun scorched some, but the rest of the seed fell on soil rich enough to produce a bountiful crop. You need to follow that example. If you send out one hundred brochures each week, make fifteen phone calls each morning, and make three office visits each afternoon, you may fail to close a deal 75 percent of the time. But the remaining 25 percent of the sales you make will still provide enough success to produce bountiful profits. Right now, you just aren't working hard enough."

I then told the man a humorous story I'd heard from my grandfather many years before. A farmer in Tennessee had a chance to buy twenty acres of scrubland near the farm he already owned. The price was very reasonable, so the farmer purchased the twenty acres. For the first two years, the farmer was too busy to do anything to the scrubland, so it produced nothing but weeds. The third year he worked extra hours and cleared the rocks from the twenty acres. Nevertheless, it produced nothing.

In the fourth year, the farmer worked extra hours and plowed under the fields for the first time. He cut back the bramble bushes, put up a white fence, and sprayed weed killer on the ground. Still, the land produced nothing.

In the fifth year, the farmer worked extra hours and fertilized the twenty acres, planted corn and tomatoes and beans, and tilled and tended the soil all summer.

That fall the farmer had his fields filled with ripe and healthy crops. A minister driving by one afternoon pulled his car to the side of the road and waved to the farmer as he worked atop his tractor. The farmer stopped the engine and climbed down from the tractor.

"I couldn't help but admire your beautiful farmland," said the minister. "Your soil is productive, your crops are bountiful, and your fields are so well tended. Isn't it amazing what God and man can do when they work together like this?"

The farmer paused for a moment, thought about that statement for a time, then responded, "Well, Parson, I s'pose that's true. But you should'a seen the place when God was workin' it by Himself."

The man I was counseling chuckled at this little story, but he also understood the message it contained; that is, no plowing, no profits. He promised me he would give careful thought to the things we had discussed.

Shortly thereafter, this same man attended a Bible study group meeting being held at my house. He arrived smiling and announced, "Things are really picking up. I signed a contract with a school to provide a month of computerized telemarketing, and I have an appointment with a financial consulting firm to make a bid on building a new computerized switchboard for its main office."

I was happy for this man. He had learned that God was his partner in all that he did, but God expected him to do his share of the work.

Proverbs 6:6 tells us to admire the hardworking ant that is never lazy. In 2 Thessalonians 3:10 Paul warns us that those who do not work should not expect God or man to provide sustenance for them.

It is honorable to work hard at whatever your calling is. This covers everything from your chosen profession to your service to Christ. An old hymn of the faith says, "Work for the night is coming, when man's work is done." Keep in mind that the work isn't done until that night comes. So, for today, roll up your sleeves.

THINKING MORE ABOUT CHAPTER 2

Scripture Verses to Ponder

> And in every work that he began in the service of the house of God, and in the law, and in the commandments, to seek his God, he did it with all his heart, and prospered.
> —2 Chronicles 31:21

> For the work of a man shall he render unto him, and cause every man to find according to his ways.
> —Job 34:11

> Then said they unto him, What shall we do, that we might work the works of God? Jesus answered and said unto them, This is the work of God, that ye believe on him whom he hath sent.
> —John 6:28–29

Let him that stole steal no more: but rather let him labour,
working with his hands the thing which is good, that he may
have to give to him that needeth.

—Ephesians 4:28

If any would not work, neither should he eat.

—2 Thessalonians 3:10

Questions to Consider

1. It has been said that God cares for the birds of the field, but He
doesn't throw the worms into the nest. Do you know many men
who have gone through life feeling that "God owed" them a living? Where do you think they developed such an idea?

2. If you were not allowed to share your faith openly with other
people while you were working at your job, what are some other
ways that you could "send a message" to your fellow employees
that Christ was the center of your life?

3. Many people are needy throughout the world, even in a nation
as prosperous as the United States. In what ways do you feel
Christians have taken positive steps to help these people? What
more could be done by individuals such as yourself?

4. Since 1965 the two-income family has become more common
than the one-income family. How has this had both positive
and negative effects on your family and on the families of your
friends, neighbors, and relatives?

5. The often quoted line, "God helps them who help themselves"
is *not* in the Bible. Nevertheless, this has been a popular saying
among people for centuries. Why do you feel people relate to
this expression so readily?

6. Do you have a personal work ethic that you live by? If not, take
a moment to create one. Write it down.

SUGGESTED ADDITIONAL READINGS

Band, William A. *Creating Value for Customers.* New York: John Wiley and Sons, 1991.

Davidow, William H., and Bro Uttal. *Total Customer Service: The Ultimate Weapon.* New York: Harper and Row, 1989.

Evans, Paul, and Fernando Bartolome. *Must Success Cost So Much?* New York: Basic Books, 1981.

Hensley, Dennis E. *Positive Workaholism.* Indianapolis: R & R Newkirk, 1983.

Juran, Joseph. *Juran on Planning for Quality.* New York: Free Press, 1988.

CHAPTER 3

SPIRITUAL HYPOXIA

And . . . he [Jesus] breathed on them, and saith unto them,
Receive ye the Holy Ghost.

—John 20:22

One of my favorite songs during the past few years has been a tune titled, "People Need the Lord." Not only is the melody beautiful, the words are also poignant. The lyrics stress the fact that Christ can help us cope with broken dreams, loneliness, and a sense of failure.

As wonderful as the message of that song is, however, it actually leaves half the story untold. A more complete song should be written titled, "People Need the Lord . . . and Most Don't Even Know It!"

Recently, for example, I was asked to meet with a man who had read one of my business books. This man was very successful financially, but as a person he felt depressed, tired, and unmotivated. He wanted me to assess his career and tell him whether he should open another store or take up yachting or do something else to get him out of his constant feeling of depression.

"If I have so many things," he asked me, "like two homes, three cars, and a private airplane, why is it my life is so empty?"

"Because *you* are," I answered. "Until you're filled with the Holy Spirit, your existence is hollow."

"What's the Holy Spirit?" he asked . . . and he meant it. For all his worldly knowledge, he knew nothing about God's plan of salvation.

This man had never attended church. He had never read the Bible. He had never had any close friends who were Christians. He desperately needed the grace and peace of Christ, but he had no way of realizing it.

I immediately recalled Romans 10:14, ". . . and how shall they believe in him of whom they have not heard? and how shall they hear without a preacher?"

Unless we share our testimonies and witness to those who are lost, they will continue to suffer and not even know what they are lacking.

Let me tell you about something that will make this even clearer to you.

When I was a newspaper reporter, I once did a feature on the training procedures for pilots in the U.S. Air Force. One of the flight conditions that a pilot must understand is hypoxia or "oxygen starvation." To demonstrate this graphically to potential pilots, the flight instructors put the students inside an altitude simulation chamber.

With oxygen masks on, the students are taken to simulated conditions of being 30,000 feet above the earth (where oxygen is very thin). The students sit in pairs. One student then removes his mask and begins to answer some very simple questions typed on a sheet of paper. He's asked to perform basic arithmetic, to circle all of the capital letters in a paragraph, to write the name of the first U.S. president, and then to write a short history of their lives.

All of the students work away busily for a few minutes. Suddenly, their partners begin to force the unclipped oxygen masks back onto the uncovered mouths and noses of the people who are writing.

After a few gulps of normal air, each writer looks down at his sheet of paper. He is astounded to discover that the first few lines he has written are very legible, but the last few lines are scribbled and totally unreadable.

The reason this is so amazing is that, just one minute earlier, the participant was absolutely sure he had written "George Washington" in perfectly legible script. For a fact, however, he was on the verge of losing consciousness. Remarkably enough, *he didn't even know he was blacking out.*

To me, this was a dramatic demonstration of the fact that there are physical conditions, like hypoxia, that a person can have without even realizing it. Unless someone else recognizes the symptoms, the victim will not get help and will go on suffering . . . even to the point of death.

Similarly, people can be spiritually starved. Unless someone, through witnessing, explains how to obtain the "breath of life" (Gen. 2:7), the lost person will never gain spiritual "consciousness."

I explained all this to the businessman who had asked to meet with me. Like a suffocating man, he seemed to be gasping for the spiritual air I had to share.

We've talked several times since then and the man's entire "atmosphere" is now different. When he accepted Christ in his life, he was given the filling of the Holy Spirit. The man is no longer empty.

He's breathing a lot easier these days.

THINKING MORE ABOUT CHAPTER 3

Scripture Verses to Ponder

> And the LORD God formed man of the dust of the ground, and breathed into his nostrils the breath of life; and man became a living soul.
>
> —Genesis 2:7

> Thus saith the Lord GOD unto these bones; Behold, I will cause breath to enter into you, and ye shall live.
>
> —Ezekiel 37:5

> And when he had said this, he breathed on them, and saith unto them, Receive ye the Holy Ghost.
>
> —John 20:22

God that made the world and all things therein, seeing that
he is Lord of heaven and earth, dwelleth not in temples made
with hands; neither is worshiped with men's hands, as though
he needed any thing, seeing he giveth to all life, and *breath,*
and all things.

—Acts 17:24–25 (emphasis added)

For what is your life? It is even a vapour, that appeareth for a
little time, and then vanisheth away.

—James 4:14

Questions to Consider

1. Have you ever been held underwater against your will by someone who was roughhousing with you in a pool or at a lake? It's a
   terrifying feeling, isn't it? Fortunately, your kicking and flailing
   make it obvious that the other person needs to let go of you,
   and, thus, you are quickly rescued. But what if the other person
   was not willing to pull you to the top? Very soon, you would die.
   That situation is occurring with people all around you who are
   drowning in sin. Have you done anything recently to pull someone to the surface?
2. Some people will tell you that "ignorance is bliss," but the man
   we read about in this story was not blissful in his ignorance of
   the Lord. Do you know any man who has wealth or fame or
   popularity, yet is miserable? If so, try to think of some ways in
   which you can witness to him.
3. Physicians and scientists tell us that many diseases, such as AIDS,
   can be present yet dormant in the human body for as long as
   ten years before they begin to tear down the immune system
   and kill a person. The lurking death is unseen, yet ever present.
   Do you know someone who is infected with sin, yet because
   this person has not evidenced immediate harm from it contin-
   ues to ignore the problem? If so, it may be prudent for you to

warn this person that the infection is terminal. This person needs to get right with God before it's too late.

SUGGESTED ADDITIONAL READINGS

Abbott, John S. C. *The History of Christianity.* Portland, Me.: George Stinson and Co., 1885.

Douglass, Stephen B., and Lee Roddy. *Making the Most of Your Mind.* San Bernardino, Calif.: Here's Life, 1983.

Foster, Richard J. *Celebration of Discipline.* New York: Harper and Row, 1978.

James, Carolyn Curtis. *When Life and Beliefs Collide.* Grand Rapids: Zondervan, 2000.

Lutzer, Erwin W. *Seven Snares of the Enemy.* Wheaton: Moody, 2000.

Thurman, Chris. *The Lies We Believe.* Nashville: Nelson, 1989.

———. *The Truths We Must Believe.* Nashville: Nelson, 1991.

CHAPTER 4

RESCUE THE PERISHING

I was born and reared in Michigan, the only state in the union that has two separate peninsulas. From 1880 through 1940 the Great Lakes handled a tremendous amount of shipping traffic. Ships took lumber, copper, and iron ore from ports in the upper peninsula and delivered these raw materials to mills and refineries in Chicago, Milwaukee, Detroit, Cleveland, Erie, and New York City.

In those days, sea captains and their pilots didn't have the sophisticated radio, radar, and sonar devices today's ships are equipped with. As such, they relied heavily on lighthouses to help them gauge distances, avoid rocks, and locate deep channels.

Many of the lighthouses were located on rocky islands or land juts on or near the shores of the upper peninsula. Families actually resided inside or next door to the lighthouse they were responsible for maintaining.

Sea storms could get violent in that area of the Great Lakes, and during each shipping season at least two or three ships would be driven into the rocks and ripped apart. The families living in the lighthouse had a specific drill they would follow whenever this happened. The father would rush to the shore and drive a heavy stake deep into the ground. He then would attach a strong rope to the stake.

With the rope secured, the family members then would wade into the water, spreading themselves about twenty-five feet apart as they wrapped an arm around the rope. The father would have a life preserver tied to the loose end of the rope, and he would swim as far out as he could.

Each time the father would see a sailor bobbing in the water, he would swim to him and encourage him to grab onto the life preserver. Then the family members would pull on the rope and bring the two men in close enough to where they could put their feet on the lake bottom. The sailor would then use the rope as a way of guiding himself to the safety of the shore. If he stumbled from exhaustion, the nearest family member would rush to his aid and help him back onto the lifeline.

In the meantime, the father would have his eldest son take the life preserver and swim out to rescue another drowning sailor, while the father regained his strength.

Many men's lives were saved this way; but, unfortunately, many men were also lost in those tempestuous waters. According to logbooks and maritime records of that era, some men died because they *refused* to be rescued. Some were blinded by the whipping waves and gave up trying to see the direction of the lighthouse. Other men became so cold and numb, they didn't believe they could hold onto the life preserver. Still others had left the sinking ship carrying their personal belongings in their waistcoats. When they refused to separate themselves from these weighty possessions, they were pulled beneath the surface and lost.

What a parallel this is to God's ever vigilant and totally dedicated effort to rescue perishing men from the depths of sin. Just as the father of the lighthouse family sent his son into the raging waters to rescue a drowning seaman, so, too, did God the Father send His Son Jesus so that "whosoever believeth in him should *not perish*, but have everlasting life" (John 3:16, emphasis added). The lifeline of salvation is still being extended. Some are grabbing hold; others, however, are not.

Metaphorically speaking, the thief on the cross was going down for the last time when Christ extended the lifeline and the thief grabbed on. That very day the thief reached the lighthouse. The second thief, however, had become so cold and numb by his wicked life, he could not believe that the lifeline would save him. As a result, he drowned in his sins (Luke 23:39–43).

Like the greedy sailors, there are also lost souls today being pulled down in sin by the weight of their worldly possessions. A rich young man approached Jesus and asked Him the secret of becoming righteous and being saved. Jesus saw that the young man was good in all areas except for his covetousness of wealth.

To free this young man from his obsession with greed, Jesus told him to give his money to the poor and thereby increase his wealth in heaven. He would then be free of the grievous weight of his money. But the young man refused to part with his worldly goods, even for the promise of salvation. He went away as heavyhearted as when he had come. He sank back under the waters of sorrow and despair (Mark 10:17–25).

Jesus tells us that He is "the light of the world: . . . [and] the light of life" (John 8:12). Those of us who have found this lighthouse now must feel burdened to extend the lifeline to those drowning in sin. The storm is raging and we can expect to be buffeted; even worse, despite our rescue efforts, many will refuse to grab the lifeline. Still, there will always be those who will "see the light" and accept our guidance to it.

For their sake, we must swim the waters.

THINKING MORE ABOUT CHAPTER 4

Scripture Verses to Ponder

> The blessing of him that was ready to *perish* came upon me: and I caused the widow's heart to sing with joy. I put on righteousness, and it clothed me: my judgment was as a robe and a diadem.
>
> —Job 29:13–14 (emphasis added)

Lord, how long wilt thou look on? *rescue* my soul from their destructions, my darling from the lions.

—Psalm 35:17 (emphasis added)

And they came to him, and awoke him, saying, Master, master, we *perish.* Then he arose, and rebuked the wind and the raging of the water: and they ceased, and there was a calm. And he said unto them, Where is your faith? And they, being afraid wondered, saying one to another, What manner of man is this! for he commandeth even the winds and water, and they obey him.

—Luke 8:24–25 (emphasis added)

The Lord is not slack concerning his promise, as some men count slackness; but is longsuffering to us-ward, not willing that any should *perish,* but that all should come to repentance.

—2 Peter 3:9 (emphasis added)

Questions to Consider

1. Some of the men we learned about in chapter 4 drowned because they were weighted down by worldly possessions. Take a moment to ask yourself, "Are there tangible things in my life that may be pulling me toward sin or may be causing me to sink to the world's baseness?" If so, what can you do about reestablishing your priorities?
2. The lighthouse served as a beacon of warning, rescue, and guidance. Christians, too, should be lighthouses. They should shine with the glory of a redeemed life. How can you be such a lighthouse in all of the areas of your life?
   • In your neighborhood:

   • On the job:

• At your church:

• In your home:

3. When the terrible storms of the Great Lakes caused the sailors to fear for their lives, the family in the lighthouse provided a safe haven for those in danger. Who do you know of who is in need of your personal assistance today? Would your kindness and help be a way of showing the love of Christ to someone in need?

SUGGESTED ADDITIONAL READINGS

Arnold, Henri. *Freedom from Sinful Thoughts: Christ Alone Breaks the Curse.* Rifton, N.Y.: Plough Publishing House, 1973.

Fuller, Cheri. *Home-Life.* Tulsa: Honor Books, 1988.

Kelsey, Morton T. *The Other Side of Silence: A Guide to Christian Meditation.* New York: Paulist Press, 1976.

Merton, Thomas. *Contemplative Prayer.* Garden City, N.Y.: Doubleday, 1969.

Schaeffer, Edith. *What Is a Family?* Old Tappan, N.J.: Revell, 1975.

CHAPTER 5

RECYCLING RIGHTEOUS RUBBISH

If you leave Highway 27 in northeastern Indiana and head toward the tiny farming village of Bryant—which isn't even marked on most maps—you'll be surprised to come upon a hidden oasis of entertainment called the Bear Creek Farms.

At Bear Creek, the clocks run slow. Bygone eras are still alive. A general store has apples in a barrel, penny candy in bins, and red long johns on the shelves. Next door, there's a vaudeville stage where barbershop quartets sing, slapstick comics wear baggy pants, and agile jugglers amaze audiences. Classic cars are on display in the parking lot, and the American flag flies in the middle of an old-fashion village square.

Best of all, Bear Creek Farms has a family-style dining room where "pass the plate" dinners feature huge platters of fried chicken, hot biscuits, mashed potatoes, and fresh vegetables. Adding to the atmosphere of this dining room are walls that are covered with all sorts of farming and household items that date as far back as pioneer days.

Part of the fun of eating at Bear Creek Farms is making a game out of trying to guess how the implements on the walls were once used. (I mistook a duck feeder one time to be a spanking machine for naughty children.)

During a recent visit to this dining room, my family members and I each took turns guessing at the function of a certain spiked rod with an auger on one end and a crank handle near the top. I thought it was some sort of posthole digger. My son thought it was part of a unicycle. My wife and daughter thought it might be something for digging up fishing worms or trapping moles.

I called the restaurant owner over and asked him to tell us about the object of our curiosity.

"Oh, that?" he said, chuckling at our guesses. "No, none of those things. Actually, this was a post that was twisted into the ground by surveyors 150 years ago, to help them measure boundaries. The surveyor sighted through his range finder while his assistant moved the pole to the correct border spot. Once the surveyor signaled that it was accurately placed, the assistant turned the handle and twisted the pole firmly into the ground. Later, fences were built from one of these poles to the next to distinguish land plots."

I was impressed. "Wow! You really know your local history," I said. "You must have rummaged through every antique store in the Midwest in order to assemble this incredible collection."

The owner smiled mischievously. "No," he said with a wink, "only through every junkyard and trash heap. You see, the only difference between an antique and a piece of rubbish is in knowing what you are looking for and then knowing what to do with it once you find it."

I quickly pulled out a pen and jotted down those words. Little did that restaurant owner know he had just provided me with an object lesson for my next week's Sunday school class.

In Philippians 3:8, Paul said, "I consider everything a loss compared to the surpassing greatness of knowing Christ Jesus my Lord, for whose sake I have lost all things. I consider them rubbish, that I may gain Christ" (NIV).

Just prior to this, Paul had presented his résumé. He had explained that he had been thoroughly educated, even to the point of becoming a scholar of the writings of Moses and the prophets ("a Pharisee"); he had not only learned Aramaic and Greek, but he had also learned to read and write Hebrew ("a Hebrew of the Hebrews"); he had come from a respected tribe (Benjamin was the tribe of Saul, the first Jewish king); and he was the son of a very respected man in the community (Acts 23:6).

Having said this, Paul then pointed out that *none* of these personal achievements had done anything to provide salvation for him. Only the acceptance of the shed blood of Christ had gained atonement for Paul. Adamantly, he stressed that his self-attained accomplishments were mere "rubbish" when compared to the *one thing* (salvation) that Christ had given him.

I'm sure that most Christians agree with and understand this stance of Paul's. However, it is the discovery of something that goes *beyond* this obvious lesson that intrigues me even more. By this I mean the discovery that God can sift through the rubbish of our lives and make use of even that. And the way He is able to do this is simply by knowing what He is looking for and then knowing what to do with it once He has found it.

This was certainly true of Paul's life. The fact that Paul could speak many languages did nothing to help bring salvation to Paul's life. Nevertheless, God used this ability of Paul's to make him the first evangelist to the Gentile nations.

Similarly, Paul's Roman citizenship was worthless in regard to securing salvation; still, God used that as a way of allowing Paul to preach to Roman leaders (Acts 26:1–2) and to convert Roman soldiers to Christianity (Phil. 4:22).

Indeed, Paul was right to label secular achievements as rubbish when compared to holy blessings; but this did not negate God's ability to put even the rubbish to good use. In fact, Isaiah said that God's eyes seek those people for whom He can make good use.

This should be an admonition to all Christians. We are not saved by works. Nevertheless, we are not saved merely to sit back and refrain from works. There is work to do for the Lord. Upon receiving salvation we are given at least one spiritual gift as a way of aiding our individual ministry. This gift can be used for the Lord, but so can our natural talents and our developed skills.

When Jesus wanted fishers of men, He recruited Peter and Andrew—
real fishermen. When Jehovah wanted a leader and ruler to guide His
people out of Egypt, He recruited Moses—a *real* prince and trained
leader. The earthly talents of these men were put to great use when
they were yielded to God.

When I look at my own life, my worldly accomplishments are mod-
est. Nevertheless, God has used my training as a college professor to
allow me to teach Sunday school. He has used my training as a journalist to allow me to write articles and books for Christian publishers.
Even though my greatest levels of secular competence are but "dirty
rags" in God's eyes, He has been able to recycle my rubbish and make
it into something righteous.

If you sometimes feel that you have very little to offer for the cause
of Christ, do this: relax and yield everything in your life to Him. Let
God do the sifting and selecting. When He spots something in your
life that He can make use of, He'll also make an opportunity available
for you to use it. At that point, you'll probably be as amazed as I was
when I was told about the function of the surveyor's marking pole.
You'll scratch your head and say, "I never would have dreamed that
that could have been used for *that!*"

THINKING MORE ABOUT CHAPTER 5

Scripture Verses to Ponder

> The LORD is my light and my salvation; whom shall I fear? the
> LORD is the strength of my life; of whom shall I be afraid?
> —Psalm 27:1

> The way of the LORD is strength to the upright: but destruction
> shall be to the workers of iniquity.
> —Proverbs 10:29

But we are all as an unclean thing, and all our righteousnesses
are as filthy rags; and we all do fade as a leaf; and our iniquities,
like the wind, have taken us away.

—Isaiah 64:6

Beat your plowshares into swords, and your pruning hooks
into spears: let the weak say, I am strong.

—Joel 3:10

I can do all things through Christ which strengtheneth me.

—Philippians 4:13

I know thy works: behold, I have set before thee an open door,
and no man can shut it: for thou hast a little strength. . . .

—Revelation 3:8

Questions to Consider

1. Have you ever gone into your garage or attic or basement to
   clear out things for spring cleaning and then found something
   precious you thought you had lost? It's fun to bring the old lamp
   back up to the living room for a while or to have some fun for
   an evening going back through the old school yearbooks. But
   what about the precious things within *yourself?* Can you redis-
   cover some talents or abilities you haven't used for a while? If
   so, maybe you can put them back into use for the Lord.
2. Although it is fun to visit museums, most people really wouldn't
   like to live in the past. It would be hard to give up microwave
   ovens, computers, telephones, and air conditioners. Nevertheless, those of us who are new creatures in Christ do have a former
   life. What did you give up when you left that life behind? Why
   would you not want to return to the "old days" of your life before your salvation experience?
3. Have you wondered sometimes why God gave you certain

talents, yet no ability in other areas? What are your talents and
how can you use them to best serve Christ?

4. Beginning with Jonah and Gideon, how many biblical charac-
   ters can you recall who felt they had no talent yet were used
   greatly by God?

SUGGESTED ADDITIONAL READINGS

Merton, Thomas. *Spiritual Direction and Meditation.* Minnesota: Li-
turgical Press, 1960.

O'Connor, Elizabeth. *Search for Silence.* Waco, Tex.: Word, 1971.

Rohrback, Peter-Thomas. *Conversation with Christ.* Chicago: Fides
Publishers, 1956.

Tozer, A. W. *The Knowledge of the Holy.* New York: Harper and Row,
1961.

Wesley, John. *Sermons on Several Occasions.* London: Epworth Press,
1971.

CHAPTER 6

MAKING CHRISTIAN
SERVICE A JOY

Several years ago, when my daughter Jeanette was only ten, she and I had the lead roles in the children's Christmas pageant at our church. I played a storekeeper and Jeanette played the youngster who worked for me. We had the time of our lives. We practiced our lines and songs together, we helped plan the designs of our costumes, and on the night of the performance we "wowed" the congregation with our presentation.

For weeks after that event, people kept coming up to me and saying, "It was such a delightful play. And you and your daughter seemed to be having such a good time performing together."

"We *were* having a good time," I responded. "That's the key to successful Christian service. Volunteer to do what you enjoy most."

That's a philosophy I've always lived by. I have given many hours of service to the Lord, and they've been pleasurable experiences because I've made it a habit to do what I enjoy, and then enjoy what I do.

During the years my son was in grades two through six, I was his youth group leader at church. Five young boys, including my Nathan, met with me each Wednesday night to memorize Scripture verses, work on crafts, read Bible stories, and play games. When Nathan became too old for the group, I resigned as a leader. I knew it wouldn't be as much fun for me as a leader if my son wasn't part of the group. I passed on my leadership to a younger dad whose son was just entering the program. I then took on a new job as the Sunday school teacher for the class my wife and I were in each week.

Whenever I sing that old-time hymn "There Is Joy in Serving Jesus," I bellow out the words. I know that joy. I have been a deacon, a lay preacher, a teacher, a youth leader, and the chairman of the school board of a Christian elementary school. I've enjoyed all these jobs. It has never been a burden for me to serve Christ in these ways; it has been a pleasure.

Conversely, if you would ever ask me to help in the nursery or lead the choir or resurface the church parking lot or offer prenuptial counseling to an engaged couple, I would turn you down flat. I either don't like to do those things or I have no abilities in those areas.

Now, you may be thinking, "Well, if everyone thinks the way he does, why, *nothing* would get done."

I don't believe that. I think everything would get done, and done very well. The apostle Paul wrote, "Now there are diversities of gifts" (1 Cor. 12:4). He explained that the Holy Spirit enables some to preach, some to teach, some to evangelize, some to give, some to help. The secret to enjoying your service to Christ is to recognize your gifts and then to use them to God's honor.

When Jesus selected His twelve disciples, He created a cooperative team. Some were scholars who could read and write; some were financial managers who could deal with money matters; some were laborers who could sail and fish, mend nets, or make tents. Together, with each man doing what he was best at, they were able to travel and spread the gospel.

Did Jesus ever ask Matthew to gather in fish? No! Did Jesus ever ask Peter to manage the group's money? No! He called them to give their *natural* talents to His service.

But then what happened? Each man who served Christ in basic ways found himself rapidly growing in talent and self-confidence as he tried new things. Peter, a roughshod fisherman, became a great preacher. Matthew, a tax collector, became a historian of Christ's life. As their talents expanded, so did their ministries. And so did their joy.

Perhaps you've wondered from time to time why God has never called you to a great ministry for Him. The answer may be that He first wants you to discover the joy of service on a beginner's level. He wants you to be part of His cooperative team, not the solo worker responsible for carrying all the burdens.

Discover your gift. Use it. Share it.

Then get ready. It won't be long before you'll discover you've been blessed with another gift.

And won't that be even *more* enjoyable!

THINKING MORE ABOUT CHAPTER 6

Scripture Verses to Ponder

> And if it seem evil unto you to serve the LORD, choose you this day whom ye will serve; whether the gods which your fathers served that were on the other side of the flood, or the gods of the Amorites, in whose land ye dwell: but as for me and my house, we will serve the LORD. And the people answered and said, God forbid that we should forsake the LORD, to serve other gods; . . . for he is our God.
> —Joshua 24:15–16, 18

> No man can serve two masters: for either he will hate the one, and love the other; or else he will hold to the one, and despise the other. Ye cannot serve God and mammon.
> —Matthew 6:24

> With good will doing service, as to the Lord, and not to men.
> —Ephesians 6:7

And whatsoever ye do, do it heartily, as to the Lord, and not
unto men; Knowing that of the Lord ye shall receive the reward
of the inheritance: for ye serve the Lord Christ.

—Colossians 3:23–24

Questions to Consider

1. Are you experiencing joy in serving Jesus in the work you are
   now doing for the Lord? If not, make a list of what you think are
   your natural talents and your spiritual gifts. Next, note ways in
   which you may be able to put these to more enjoyable use for
   Christ.

My Talent or Gift	Its Use for the Lord
[Example] *A good voice*	*Join the church choir/sing a solo.*
A.	
B.	
C.	

2. Zacchaeus and Levi (Matthew) were both wealthy men, but both
   left their jobs as tax collectors to follow Jesus. What does this
   tell us about the old adage that money cannot buy happiness?
3. Have you ever felt as if you were tricked into accepting a job at
   church that you didn't want? Did someone try to make you feel
   guilty about saying no? You probably didn't do as well at that
   job as someone who is skilled in that area could have done. So,
   how will you handle this situation if or when it comes up again?

SUGGESTED ADDITIONAL READINGS

Davidson, Jeff. *Breathing Space: Living and Working at a Comfortable Pace in a Sped-Up Society.* New York: MasterMedia, 1991.

Engstrom, Ted. *The Making of a Christian Leader.* Grand Rapids: Zondervan, 1976.

Hensley, Dennis E., and Holly G. Miller. *How to Stop Living for the Applause: Help for Women Who Need to Be Perfect.* Ann Arbor: Servant, 1990.

Walas, Kathleen, and Gail Blanke. *Taking Control of Your Life.* New York: MasterMedia, 1990.

CHAPTER 7

PRAYERS FOR THE SICK
WHY THEY ARE AND SOMETIMES *Aren't* ANSWERED

I have spent most of my professional life as a journalist. I also hold a Ph.D. in English. Hence, I'm a pragmatist, a realist, a researcher, and a documentor. I deal in verifiable facts, not speculations, dreams, wishes, or assumptions.

Having said that, I now tell you that twice in my life I have witnessed outright miracles. By miracles, I mean acts of God that radically altered normal, physical laws of nature. Both of these miracles were in direct response to prayer and both were related to physical afflictions.

I do not believe in faith healing in modern times. I believe that the gift of miraculous healing was given only to the apostles and a few other designated disciples for a limited time and only as a way of verifying their authenticity as spokesmen for Christ.

I strongly believe, however, that the book of James tells us we should pray for the power of God to intercede in hastening the normal recovery time of people who are ill. To that end, I pray frequently for people I know who are battling illnesses and diseases or are recovering from injuries.

For many years I wrestled with a question that I'm sure most other

Christians have wondered about, too. Why, I asked myself, is it that God seems to respond to prayers for the recovery of some people, yet not for others?

Consider, for example, this situation. Some years ago I was serving as a deacon in a rural church in Indiana. A seven-year-old girl named Gretta Kotke was deaf in her right ear. Physicians had told Gretta's parents that the bones of her inner ear were malformed at birth. Using several x-rays, the doctors showed Mr. and Mrs. Kotke the problems and explained that there was a delicate, somewhat risky operation that could be performed that might correct part of the problem.

The Kotkes put off the operation, not wanting to put their daughter at any risk. When Gretta was in second grade, however, it was harder for her to hear her teacher and to keep up in her studies. With great apprehension, Gretta's parents decided to let the doctors operate on her ear. New sets of x-rays showed that the condition was the same as it had been since birth. The operation was scheduled for a Monday morning.

On the Sunday prior to the day of the operation, Mr. Kotke (who was a seminary student at the time) asked six elders of the church to meet with him and his daughter in one of the church's classrooms. He asked the men to pray over his daughter, invoking the power of God to help Gretta receive hearing in her ear through this operation. We prayed earnestly, asking God to guide the doctors, to heal Gretta, to comfort the entire family, and for God to work His perfect will in Gretta's life.

The following morning, Gretta woke up and told her parents she could hear out of both ears. The Kotkes thought that Gretta might be afraid of the operation and, as such, might be trying to make them feel she didn't need it. When they arrived at the hospital, however, a final set of x-rays was made, and to the total astonishment of the doctors, Gretta's ear was perfect. The malformed bones had become normal. A hearing test followed and confirmed that Gretta could hear as well out of her right ear as she could out of her left. The doctors sent her home. The operation was canceled.

Today, Gretta's father, the Rev. Kevin Kotke, is senior pastor of a large church in Indianapolis. Gretta is now in high school and still has perfect hearing. Each time I see Pastor Kotke, we always recall the way Gretta's ear was miraculously healed, and we praise the Lord for it. Kevin has told me that that event has enabled him time and again to offer hope and comfort through testimony and prayer to many other parents in his congregation who have children who are ill or injured. The tragedy of Gretta's illness and the miracle of her recovery seem to have been part of God's preparation of Kevin for his ministry.

GOD'S USE OF ILLNESS

I can relate well to Kevin's experience, not only because I was there to witness it, but because I had also had an equally miraculous incident occur in my own daughter's life.

On August 19, 1978, when my wife went to the hospital to give birth to our second child, we were told by our doctors that they could no longer hear the baby's heartbeat and that the fetal monitor was not registering a heartbeat for the baby. The child, they told us, had died in the womb.

We were emotionally crushed by the news. Our friends from church hurried to the hospital to be with us. While the doctors gave my wife medications to induce labor, I retreated to the hospital chapel where my church friends and I prayed for my wife's health and for God's grace to sustain us in our grief.

A few hours later I went into the delivery room with my wife so that the deceased infant could be removed from her. Just prior to this, I had been asked to sign a form allowing the doctors to perform an autopsy after delivery. My hand had shaken as I'd signed it.

When our daughter was born, an immediate examination was given and the doctor thought he detected a very faint heartbeat. A tube was inserted down the throat of the baby and a hand pump was used to breathe for the child. Our baby was rushed by special ambulance sixty miles away to the intensive care unit of Riley Children's Hospital in Indianapolis. It was discovered there that the child had been born with a complete heart block, but with proper medical attention she had an excellent chance of living.

Back in Muncie, I questioned the attending doctors. Why hadn't they heard the baby's heartbeat? They had no answer. Why hadn't the fetal monitor—an extremely sensitive pulse detector—registered the baby's heartbeat? Again, the doctors had no answer.

"We had four doctors check your wife," one of the physicians told me, "and it was the unanimous decision that the baby was dead. I, myself, cannot believe she is alive. I've never seen anything like this before."

A few weeks later we were able to take our daughter home. Today, she is a freshman in college and an honor roll student. Her heart beats at half the normal rate, but she has never had to have heart surgery nor to rely on medications. To my mind, she came back from the dead as a newborn.

There is one more part to this story, however. One year after my wife and I had endured the tragedy of what we thought was the death of our baby, the physician who had cared for my wife during her pregnancy lost a child of her own. Dr. Nancy Griffith gave birth to a son named Patrick who was born with multiple birth disorders. He lived just three days.

Dr. Griffith was terribly distraught. She not only felt a mother's loss of her child, she also felt the frustration of being a physician who could not heal her son.

Word got back to me of Dr. Griffith's depression and of how she would not be comforted by friends and family members. I knew what her problem was. She felt that no one else could really relate to her sense of loss. I, however, knew that I could relate, because my wife and I had been through it.

I wrote Nancy a long letter that proved I knew how and what she was thinking and feeling. I shared specific passages of Scripture with her that had become precious to me as a parent. I reinforced her self-esteem by assuring her that she had been a marvelous help to my wife during her prenatal care months.

Additionally, I told Nancy very honestly that the loss of her son might seem like unanswered prayer, but it might be God's way of sensitizing her heart so that for the remainder of her long career as a physician she would have *firsthand knowledge* of the grief and worry parents experience over the sickness of a child. This depth of understanding on her part would make her a very effective family physician.

Nancy was greatly comforted by my letter. It gave her new hope, new insights on her ordeal, and new energy to return to her career. In subsequent years, she has given birth to other children and has also maintained a successful medical practice. Her patients say she is one of the most caring, sensitive, and concerned doctors they've ever known.

A BIBLICAL PERSPECTIVE

So, we see that Gretta Kotke's medical ordeal enabled her father to become a more effective pastor. My daughter Jeanette's medical ordeal enabled me to be a comfort to Dr. Nancy Griffith. The loss of Dr. Griffith's child enabled her to become a more effective physician.

Am I saying that these are the reasons why these events transpired? No. I can't know that for sure. However, I can say that within the providence of God's perfect will, something good came out of each of these ordeals (Rom. 8:28).

I can also say that God does use sickness as a way of preparing us for ministry. Second Corinthians 1:3–4 says, in part, that "God . . . comforts us in all our affliction so that we may be able to comfort those who are in any affliction with the comfort with which we ourselves are comforted by God" (NASB).

These words were written by the apostle Paul, who prayed fervently many times, asking God to remove a physical disorder from Paul's body. God did not grant that request, so Paul accepted the will of God and continued his ministry.

I cannot say specifically why God chose not to heal Paul. I can note one thing, however. When Paul's disorder became worse, he sent for Luke "the beloved physician" to travel with him. From this experience,

Luke produced the book of Luke and the book of Acts in our New Testament. These two books alone provide Christians with the story of Christ's life on earth and the lives of the apostles. Something marvelous was produced as the result of Paul's infirmity . . . and simultaneously Luke became a more sensitive doctor and Christian in the process.

What we see then, in summary, is that the question as to why one person is healed because of prayer and another is not has been asked for centuries. With perspective, however, we are able to realize that God's plan for our lives can be fulfilled *either way*. Miraculous recoveries can lead to great ministries, but so can prolonged illnesses or even the death of a loved one. Accepting this on faith is a great step in our Christian development.

THINKING MORE ABOUT CHAPTER 7

Scripture Verses to Ponder

> The LORD will strengthen him upon the bed of languishing: thou wilt make all his bed in his sickness.
> —Psalm 41:3

> They have stricken me, shalt thou say, and I was not sick; they have beaten me, and I felt it not: when shall I awake? I will seek it yet again.
> —Proverbs 23:35

> When the evening was come, they brought unto him many that were possessed with devils: and he cast out the spirits with his word, and healed all that were sick: That it might be fulfilled which was spoken by Esaias [Isaiah] the prophet, saying, Himself took our infirmities, and bare our sicknesses.
> —Matthew 8:16–17

And the prayer of faith shall save the sick, and the Lord shall raise him up; and if he have committed sins, they shall be forgiven him. Confess your faults one to another, and pray one for another, that ye may be healed. The effectual fervent prayer of a righteous man availeth much.

—James 5:15–16

Questions to Consider

1. Can you look back on a time when you were forced to lie bed-ridden for an extended period of time because of illness? What went through your mind during this time? What lessons did you learn from this experience? What words of comfort would you share with someone else who was going through a similar situation?
2. The Bible teaches, "Whatsoever ye sow, that shall ye also reap." Can you think of past sin in your life or someone else's life that has caused suffering later in life?
3. Peter tells us that Christians sometimes bring their problems upon themselves by straying from the path of righteousness and willfully going the way of the world (1 Peter 2:20). Can you think of a time in your life when this occurred to you or perhaps to someone else you know? What is the obvious lesson from that?
4. The apostle Paul prayed to have a physical affliction removed from him, yet God chose not to release Paul from this problem. Later, Paul said that the weaker he became, the more he became dependent on God; and this dependence gave him God's strength and, thus, made him stronger than ever. Is this level of faith too high for you to comprehend? Do you know anyone who suffers greatly from a physical affliction yet serves the Lord in effective ways? (Suggestion: Consider people in history, such as John Milton, the blind poet who wrote *Paradise Lost,* or contemporary people such as artist Joni Eareckson Tada.)

Suggested Additional Readings

Bonhoeffer, Dietrich. *The Way to Freedom.* New York: Harper and Row, 1966.

Bounds, E. M. *Power Through Prayer.* Chicago: Moody, n.d.

Radcliffe, Lynn J. *Making Prayer Real.* New York: Abingdon-Cokesbury Press, 1952.

Sanford, Agnes. *The Healing Gifts of the Spirit.* New York: Lippincott, 1966.

Underhill, Evelyn. *Practical Mysticism.* New York: E. P. Dutton and Co., 1943.

CHAPTER 8

I CAN READ YOU
LIKE A BOOK

Like all little boys, I used to love it when my mom would whip up a batch of homemade cookies. I especially liked chocolate chip and oatmeal raisin. If I was running in the backyard or playing in the basement, I'd get a whiff of those freshly baked cookies and I'd make a beeline to the kitchen.

"You can have one cookie now," my mother would say, "but that's all before supper. I'll pack the rest of these in your school lunches all week."

One cookie only served to whet my appetite. Sometimes I would wait until my mother went into another room and then I'd sneak into the cookie jar and grab a few more.

Half an hour later, when I sat at the dinner table just pushing the corn and meat around on my plate, my mother would say, "You got into the cookie jar, didn't you, young man?"

I'd look up, trying to appear shocked that she would even think such a thing of me. Before I could deny it, she'd say, "I know that look of yours. I can read you like a book. You've got guilt written all over your face. Finish your dinner and go straight to bed."

I would later examine my face. I'd wonder what creases in my forehead, what dimples in my cheeks, what folds in my neck had contorted to form the word "guilt." Never would the word manifest itself for me, no matter how I squinted my eyes, puffed my cheeks, or pursed my lips. Nevertheless, for my mother, the word would emblazon itself on my face in neon each time I broke a house rule.

Many years later, when I was in high school, I became very close to a foreign exchange student who attended our school for a year. When the student returned to Germany, I was heartsick. I tried to act as though it didn't matter, but my mom saw through me.

"I can read you like a book, Son," she told me one afternoon, putting a consoling arm around me. "You really miss your friend, don't you? I know you're trying to go on as usual, but I can read your expressions. You're really lonely. So, I'll tell you what: let's go downtown and get some travel brochures. As part of your high school graduation present, maybe Dad and I can help send you on a trip to Germany next summer."

My whole attitude changed after that. I was a new person. I had something special to look forward to and, sure enough, a year later I made the trip.

I'm now in my mid-fifties, but whenever I get back home for a visit, I have the feeling my mom still can read me like a book. She seems to ask just the right questions about my work, my family, and my church activities. She gets me talking about the most important things in my life at that moment. I don't know, maybe now that I have more wrinkles it may be even easier to read my face than when I was a kid. Whatever the situation, my mom's still good at it.

The Bible warns us that our mothers aren't the only people who can read us like a book. For a fact, many people are "reading" us, determining from our words and deeds and behavior what sort of people we are, what we stand for, and what we believe in.

Paul wrote to the Christians at Corinth, "You are our letter, written in our hearts, known and read by all men; being manifested that you are a letter of Christ, cared for by us, written not with ink, but with the Spirit of the living God, not on tablets of stone, but on tablets of human hearts" (2 Cor. 3:2–3 NASB).

Sometimes it can be beneficial to have people "read" us, as was the case when my mother helped me deal with the loneliness of my friend's departure. Other times, however, when people read in us that we are the type of person who sneaks into the cookie jar, it can be embarrassing to be so transparent.

The lesson in all this is obvious: Like it or not, as Christians we are walking billboards; we are living books; people are going to read us every day. Our message is engraved on our hearts and determines the "plot" of our life stories.

What sort of author are you? Have you carefully crafted and edited and printed the words of your life story so that they create a best-seller among people who read you? When you aren't around, are your reviews good? Do people want a copy of you?

Paul said, "For to me to live is Christ" (Phil. 1:21). The text of his life was a reprint of the teachings of Christ. To that end, he desired for people to read him.

Do you desire for people to read you? Is your life an open book? It should be. After all, you may be the only Bible some people ever read.

THINKING MORE ABOUT CHAPTER 8

Scripture Verses to Ponder

> O LORD, thou hast searched me, and known me. Thou knowest my downsitting and mine uprising, thou understandest my thought afar off. Thou compassest my path and my lying down, and art acquainted with all my ways. For there is not a word in my tongue, but, lo, O LORD, thou knowest it altogether.
> —Psalm 139:1–4

> Understanding is a wellspring of life unto him that hath it.
> —Proverbs 16:22

And he that searcheth the hearts knoweth what is the mind of the Spirit, because he maketh intercession for the saints according to the will of God.

—Romans 8:27

. . . for the Spirit searcheth all things, yea, the deep things of God.

—1 Corinthians 2:10

Questions to Consider

1. How do you decide when to inject yourself into another person's problems? If you have a family member or a close friend whom you can "read like a book" and you know that this person is deeply troubled by some matter, how do you go about approaching this person with an offer of help?

2. Personally, do you find it easy or difficult to accept help from others? Are you the sort of person who keeps everything bottled up inside, fearful that if you told your problems to someone else, the "word might get out" about you? Or, conversely, do you have a friend you can turn to, someone who can "read you" and know how to help you?

3. Has it ever happened in your life that someone else knew more about your emotional state than you did? Has someone ever approached you and told you that you seem "bothered" by something and, upon consideration, you realized that there *was* something that you needed to deal with? Such friends are wonderful, for they "read us right" and help us to keep our balance in life.

4. What important lessons have you learned from people in your life who have been able to "read you" accurately?
   • Your parents:
   • Your siblings:
   • Your friends:

SUGGESTED ADDITIONAL READINGS

Fénelon, François. *Christian Perfection.* Minneapolis: Bethany, 1975.

Gish, Arthur G. *Beyond the Rat Race.* New Canaan, Conn.: Keats, 1973.

Jackson, Dave and Neta. *Living Together in a World Falling Apart.* Carol Stream, Ill.: Creation House, 1974.

à Kempis, Thomas. *The Imitation of Christ.* New York: Pyramid Publications, 1967.

Sider, Ronald J. *Rich Christians in an Age of Hunger.* Downers Grove, Ill.: InterVarsity, 1977.

CHAPTER 9

THE PREPAID DEBT

It came as a total shock to my wife and me when we heard the news that the son of two of our oldest and dearest friends had been arrested on a charge of grand theft. The boy had stolen a car and had robbed a store in order to get money to buy illegal drugs to support an addiction he had developed.

After a quick trial, the young man was sentenced to three years in a medium-security state prison. He was only sixteen years old, and his parents had not known of his problems with alcohol and drugs until after he was arrested. The other children in the family were, and still are, excellent students and fine citizens.

I'm pleased to say that, after having finished his first year in prison, this young man has taken major steps to turn his life around. He has completed a high school equivalency program, he has taken up physical conditioning, and he has drawn closer to the Lord through prayer and Bible study.

When this young man was first put in prison, nearly all of his friends and most of his relatives who were not in his immediate family turned their backs on him. They didn't write to him or visit him in prison or call his parents to ask about him. They wanted nothing more to do with him.

I, on the other hand, began to bombard this young man with mail. I sent him letters, cartoons, jokes, copies of articles I had written, church bulletins, and passages of Scripture. He answered as often as he could, but whether he wrote or not, I continued to send mail to him.

Just recently, I received a letter from this young man in which he told me he was going to be considered for a reduced sentence because of his good conduct and change of attitude. He thanked me profusely for being such a great source of encouragement to him during those first lonely, terrifying months in prison. Near the end of his letter he wrote, "I cannot think of one good reason why you should have been so kind and so caring. I am so unworthy. I've never done a single thing to warrant such concern on your part. I owe you a debt so deep, I'll never be able to repay it."

To this young man's surprise, I wrote back and told him that his dad had paid his debt for him five years before he was born. I explained that during the 1970s I had become seriously ill one summer. I was hospitalized for two weeks and then was confined to bed rest at home for the remainder of the summer.

During those months, this young man's father had gone above and beyond the call of duty to care for me. He visited me four or five times each week. He brought in hot meals for my wife and me. He ran errands, brought us newspapers, told me jokes, and made me laugh. He read the Bible to me and prayed for me. I'm totally convinced that his concern for me greatly hastened my recovery.

I was very grateful to this man. Yet, I wondered if I would ever be able to repay this great debt of kindness. Then, more than twenty years later when this man's son was put in prison, I immediately thought of the Old Testament story of David and Mephibosheth, and saw my opportunity.

Kind David had dearly loved his boyhood friend Jonathan. Although Jonathan was King Saul's son and was the natural heir to the throne of Israel, he relinquished his claim to the kingship when God's prophet Samuel anointed David instead. Jonathan saved David's life on more than one occasion when David was a hunted man. David continually felt sincere gratitude to his friend.

After Jonathan was killed in battle, David wanted to honor his friend's memory. He found out that Jonathan had a teenage son named Mephibosheth who was lame in both legs. David had Mephibosheth brought to him and told him, "I will surely shew thee kindness for Jonathan thy father's sake, and will restore thee all the land of Saul thy father; and thou shalt eat bread at my table continually" (2 Sam. 9:7).

Mephibosheth was overwhelmed by this generosity. He replied to David that he was totally unworthy of such benevolence. He referred to himself as a dead dog. What he did not understand, however, was that when David looked at Mephibosheth, he did not see a pathetic little crippled boy. He saw only the image of Jonathan. To David, Mephibosheth's debt had been paid long before the boy had ever been born.

What a marvelous parallel this is to the relationship we have with God, our heavenly Father. One day when we transcend this life in the flesh, we will be ushered into the King's presence. A special place will have been prepared for us (John 14:2). It will be so grand and glorious, we will know that nothing we have ever done will have merited such a reward. We will feel a great sense of indebtedness.

But that will not change things.

For those of us who have received Christ as Savior and have accepted His shed blood as the atonement for our sins, the debt will be prepaid. The Father will look at us, but He will only see the image of Jesus. He will welcome us at His table forever.

And our only justification for being there will be the fact that *someone else* paid our debt for us long before we were ever born.

THINKING MORE ABOUT CHAPTER 9

Scripture Verses to Ponder

> Give us this day our daily bread. And forgive us our debts, as we forgive our debtors.
>
> —Matthew 6:11–12

The servant therefore fell down, and worshipped him, saying, Lord, have patience with me, and I will pay thee all. Then the lord of that servant was moved with compassion, and loosed him, and forgave him the debt.

—Matthew 18:26–27

But a certain Samaritan, as he journeyed, came where he was: and when he saw him, he had compassion on him, And went to him, and bound up his wounds, pouring in oil and wine, and set him on his own beast, and brought him to an inn, and took care of him. And on the morrow when he departed, he took out two pence, and gave them to the host, and said unto him, Take care of him; and whatsoever thou spendest more, when I come again, I will repay thee.

—Luke 10:33–35

Questions to Consider

1. Two men were debating the merits of personal service to the local church. The first man explained that he spent an average of twelve hours each week attending church, going to choir practice, preparing a Sunday school lesson, and visiting the sick. The second man said he only attended church on Sunday morning and evening, but because he spent all of the other time involved in his business, he was able to contribute five times more money to the church than the first man. Were the men of equal service to their local church? Why or why not?

2. How many times have people done a favor for you or helped you during a difficult time in your life without expecting any payment in return? Have you expressed your gratitude to these people? Have you made yourself ready to be at their side should trouble befall them?

3. An old hymn of the faith proclaims, "Jesus paid it all; all to him I owe; sin had left a crimson stain; he washed it white as snow."

When is the last time you thanked Christ for paying the debt
you could not pay for yourself?
4. The national debt in America now ranges in the trillions of dol-
   lars. The savings and loan failures of the 1980s nearly broke the
   national budget. Presidents Carter, Reagan, Bush, and Clinton
   all tried to reduce government spending, but with no success.
   Isn't it comforting to know that even though our earthly debts
   are out of control, our heavenly debts are paid in full? In God's
   eyes, you are debt free.

SUGGESTED ADDITIONAL READINGS

Bonhoeffer, Dietrich. *The Cost of Discipleship.* New York: Macmillan,
    1959.
Hensley, Dennis E. *How to Manage Your Money: Financial Strategies
    for Christians.* Anderson, Ind.: Warner Press, 1989.
————. *Money Wise: Honoring God with Creative Money Management.*
    Eugene, Ore.: Harvest House, 1991.
Brother Lawrence. *The Practice of the Presence of God.* Nashville: Up-
    per Room Publishing, 1950.
Peck, John, and Charles Strohmer. *Uncommon Sense: God's Wisdom
    for Our Complex and Changing World.* Sevierville, Tenn.: Master
    Press, 2000.
Yoder, John Howard. *The Politics of Jesus.* Grand Rapids: Eerdmans,
    1972.

CHAPTER 10

THE HOUSE OF GOD

And Jesus said, . . . This day is salvation come to this house.
—Luke 19:9

On a side wall in the foyer of our home, we have a plaque hanging at eye level. On it is printed Joshua 24:15, ". . . as for me and my house, we will serve the LORD."

A mailman came into our home recently to deliver a package. He noticed the plaque and said, "Hey! I'm a believer, too. I wish you had that plaque mounted on the outside of your house. It would make me smile each time I drove past your place."

After he left, I began to think about how so many of my neighbors were making statements about their beliefs and their life priorities by the way they adorned the outside of their homes.

One neighbor had a flagpole that flew his college flag each time the school won an athletic event. A lady across the street kept her "first prize" sign in her yard a full month after winning the city's "Yard Beautification Award." An elderly couple down the street, fearful of being robbed, had their door and windows covered with warning signs about their electronic security system.

You could tell a lot about the people inside the houses just by looking at the houses themselves.

God's people have adorned their homes in ways that have identified themselves as His children. During the tenth plague before the Exodus, the Jews spread lamb's blood over their doorways to show obedience to God. During the New Testament era, Christians used to draw a symbol of a fish on their homes to identify themselves as Christians to other believers.

Today, however, as my mailman pointed out, we have few if any outward signs to denote that ours are homes where God is honored. And that's unfortunate, because the Bible tells us that the home plays a vital role in God's plan for mankind.

If a home is to endure, it must be God-honoring.

Proverbs 12:7 tells us that only "the house of the righteous shall stand." This is more evident today than ever. The ever-increasing number of runaway children, unwed mothers, teenage suicides, and broken marriages shows a lack of righteousness in the modern family structure. To be apart from God's will for proper family development is to invite problems and disorder.

Also to endure, a house must have family unity. In Mark 3:25 we read, "And if a house be divided against itself, that house cannot stand." Unity is developed when there is a sense of organization. Parents must accept responsibility for the nurture and care of their children, and children are obligated to honor their parents. When children are allowed to show disrespect for their parents, it leads to disobedience and rebellion. Soon, there is no sense of direction in the family. The home disintegrates as each person goes off in independent directions. God's plan, however, calls for the family members to contribute to and benefit from the support of the others.

Additionally, the home is to be a place where reverence for God is emphasized. First Timothy 5:4 explains that children are to "learn first to show piety at home." Praying before bed and at mealtimes is something children learn quickly and enjoy doing. Maintaining family devotions, in which family members take turns reading Scripture and sharing life experiences, helps to develop a natural harmony with God.

A family that makes God a part of its daily activities is a family that both respects and trusts in God.

Beyond meeting the needs of the immediate family, the home also should strive to meet the spiritual and personal needs of fellow believers. The book of Acts tells us that in its beginning stages, the church body took turns meeting in various members' homes. These Christians ate meals together (2:46), praised God together, and studied the teachings of Jesus together (5:42). There was abundant fellowship and great evidence of spiritual growth. Today, Christians continue to enjoy opening their homes to each other for home Bible studies, Sunday dinners, and other times of fellowship. It's a tradition worth keeping.

What about your home? Have you ever stopped to consider whether or not the appearance of your home offers any evidence of what goes on inside?

During the Great Depression thousands of unemployed men rode boxcars from town to town seeking food, shelter, and a bit of work. These hobos marked their trails with a series of symbols that would help them and other vagrants know what kind of home they were approaching.

If a hobo drew a circled x on a picket fence or on the side of a home, it meant "this is a good place to get a handout." Two curved lines over a circle meant "you can sleep in the barn here." Lines that resembled a fence meant "watch out for dogs or a loose bull at this farm." A cross meant "this is a godly family—watch your language and show respect for God."

Consider this: if, instead of a hobo, God were to send an angel to put a mark on your home, what would the sign be? Would it be a fish, a cross, and lamb's blood . . . or would it be the solitary word "Icabod," meaning God's glory has departed from this place (1 Sam. 4:21)?

Jesus made it a practice to visit homes. He went to the houses of Peter, Lazarus, Zacchaeus, Matthew, Simon the Pharisee, and countless others. He wants to come into your house, too. He has said, "Behold, I stand at the door, and knock: if any man hear my voice, and open the door, I will come in to him . . ." (Rev. 3:20).

I like to think that Jesus is so much a part of our house, He doesn't even bother to knock. He just walks in and says, "Hi, everybody. I'm home."

THINKING MORE ABOUT CHAPTER 10

Scripture Verses to Ponder

> Thus saith the LORD, Set thine house in order: for thou shalt die, and not live.
>
> —Isaiah 38:1

> And if a house be divided against itself, that house cannot stand.
>
> —Mark 3:25

> Howbeit Jesus suffered him not, but saith unto him, Go home to thy friends, and tell them how great things the Lord hath done for thee, and hath had compassion on thee.
>
> —Mark 5:19

> For if a man know not how to rule his own house, how shall he take care of the church of God?
>
> —1 Timothy 3:5

> But if any widow have children or nephews, let them learn first to shew piety at home, and to requite their parents: for that is good and acceptable before God.
>
> —1 Timothy 5:4

Questions to Consider

1. Have you ever taken an inventory of the rooms of your house to see if there are any "signs" that yours is a house that loves and

honors God? Take a moment to look at the books, pictures, and other items in each room. What is God-honoring?
  • kitchen
  • living room
  • dining room
  • bedroom
  • den/family room
  • basement
  • foyer/hallways

2. Do you pay attention to signs on people's cars (bumper stickers, window IDs, rearview mirror hangings)? People spend a lot of time in their automobiles in today's mobile society. Is your car a positive or negative statement of your testimony?

3. Real estate agents always suggest to people who are selling their homes that they should bake bread on the day of an open house. This gives the home an aroma of something good and wholesome. What is it that people sense when they enter your home? Is there an immediate sensation that this is a wholesome dwelling maintained by a godly family?

4. Have you ever had a brother or sister or a son or daughter who has gone away on vacation or to college and then come back home? How is the house "different" in both instances?

SUGGESTED ADDITIONAL READINGS

Bonhoeffer, Dietrich. *The Cost of Discipleship.* New York: Macmillan, 1963.

Otto, Donna. *All in Good Time.* Nashville: Nelson, 1985.

Steere, Douglas. *On Beginning from Within.* New York: Harper and Brothers, 1943.

Thurman, Chris. *If Christ Were Your Counselor.* Nashville: Nelson, 1993.

Trueblood, Elton. *The Humor of Christ.* New York: Harper and Row, 1964.

CHAPTER 11

DRIFTING WITHOUT
DIRECTION

A few years ago a Detroit family went to the shores of Lake Huron for a weekend of camping. While the parents were busy setting up the campsite, the family's two teenage girls took their inflatable air mattresses to the shore and stretched out on them in shallow water.

The air was warm, the setting was peaceful, and the water was relaxing. Both girls dozed off. While asleep, they were carried on a receding tide from the shore into the deeper, colder, rougher water. By the time the girls awoke, they were in a perilous situation. They screamed, but no one heard them. They kicked and paddled, but the tide (known as a *seiche*) was too strong for them to overcome. The cold water began to make their legs and hands numb.

Finally, the girls' father came to the shoreline and frantically searched for his daughters with his binoculars. He spotted them, far out on the lake, being thrashed by huge waves. In a matter of minutes both girls dropped from their air mattresses and sank to their deaths as the father watched helplessly.

The next day a newspaper article regarding the incident used the headline, "Directionless Drifting Drowns Daughters." Besides providing information about the accident, the article offered water safety tips to prevent similar accidents that summer.

SPIRITUAL DRIFTING

The Bible contains several "newspaper articles" that report the spiritual drifting of individuals who eventually drowned in the deep waters of sin. In a letter to the Colossians, for example, the apostle Paul mentioned a faithful companion named Demas (Col. 4:14). Two years later, however, Paul wrote to Timothy, saying, "Demas hath forsaken me, having loved this present world, and is departed unto Thessalonica" (2 Tim. 4:10). Demas apparently began to drift away from his Christian faith during that two-year period and, in time, wound up in the deep waters of worldliness.

Similarly, in Revelation 2:12–17, we read of the church at Pergamus. For a long time this church had been a haven of spiritual purity in a region that was described as "Satan's seat." In time, however, its members drifted from the shores of sound doctrine. They began to blend pagan religious practices, such as eating food that had been sacrificed to idols, with Christian practices. Ultimately, they couldn't tell the difference between what was God-honoring and what was blasphemous. As a result, Christ warned that He was at the point of eradicating the entire church.

In both of these examples, the drifting occurred so gradually, the people were no more aware of it than the two girls in Detroit had been aware of the fact that they were drifting into the deep waters of Lake Huron. We have no record to indicate that either Demas or the congregation at Pergamus "woke up" in time to prevent themselves from drowning in sin.

SECURING THE ANCHOR

The Bible teaches us many ways we can keep from drifting into sin. First, we are taught to use our trust in God as "an anchor of the soul"

(Heb. 6:19). Our faith, obedience, and trust in God keeps our souls secured and steadfast the same way a huge anchor keeps a ship secured and steadfast. No storms of life are strong enough to drag the anchor of God from its position of holding us steadfastly in His love and protection.

Second, we must keep our eyes focused on Jesus so that if we should ever start to drift or sink, we can immediately reach out and grab His rescuing hands. When Peter left his boat and walked across the water to go to Jesus, he was safe. However, when Peter took his eyes off the Lord and began to concentrate on the wind and water around him, he sank (Matt. 14:30). Likewise, we should constantly focus on Jesus rather than concentrate on the worldly things around us. Through prayer and Bible study we can maintain our proper bearing. Jesus is our focal point and our lighthouse.

Third, we must chart a proper course for our voyage through life. When God told Jonah to go to Ninevah, Jonah instead sailed in the opposite direction to Tarshish. God used the natural elements of wind and waves to show His displeasure with Jonah. Jonah was thrown from the ship and swallowed by a great fish. In time, he made his journey to Ninevah (Jonah 3:3–4) and he did God's bidding there. Today, if we elect to flee from God's call and, instead, to sail on the seas of worldliness, we can expect to experience spiritual, emotional, and psychological storms. We, too, may find ourselves going "overboard" and sinking. God's course, however, avoids the storms.

Fourth, we must be sure that our vessel is seaworthy. Had the two girls in Detroit fallen asleep in a yacht or motorboat, they could have made it back to shore from deep water. Their flimsy air mattresses, however, were not made to withstand big waves and a strong undertow.

When Noah built the ark, he fitted the wood pieces together and then made them doubly airtight by covering both the inside and outside of the hull with tar (Gen. 6:14). The ark took approximately one hundred years to build, was nearly the size of a smaller World War II aircraft carrier (450 feet long), and had the water tonnage displacement of a modern Ohio-class nuclear submarine (20,000 tons of water). While the whole earth was laid waste, the ark suffered no damage. Now, that's being seaworthy!

Our bodies are our vessels (1 Thess. 4:4). If we keep them sanctified, honorable, and righteous, they will remain waterproof even when the worst storms of life rage against us.

So, as we see, the elements of running a tight ship for the Lord are explained to us throughout the Bible: (1) let God be the anchor of our souls; (2) let Jesus serve as our lighthouse; (3) let God's direction serve to chart our course; and (4) let our vessels always be shipshape in all aspects of godliness. With this sort of seaworthiness, we'll never drift away from God.

THINKING MORE ABOUT CHAPTER 11

Scripture Verses to Ponder

> And Peter answered him and said, Lord, if it be thou, bid me come unto thee on the water. And he said, Come. And when Peter was come down out of the ship, he walked on the water, to go to Jesus. But when he saw the wind boisterous, he was afraid; and beginning to sink, he cried, saying, Lord, save me. And immediately Jesus stretched forth his hand, and caught him, and said unto him, O thou of little faith, wherefore didst thou doubt? And when they were come into the ship, the wind ceased.
> —Matthew 14:28–32

> For this is the will of God, even your sanctification, that ye should abstain from fornication: That every one of you should know how to possess his vessel in sanctification and honour.
> —1 Thessalonians 4:3–4

> God, willing more abundantly to shew unto the heirs of promise the immutability of his counsel, confirmed it by an oath: That by two immutable things, in which it was impossible for God to lie, we might have a strong consolation, who have fled for refuge to lay hold upon the hope set before

us: Which hope we have *as an anchor of the soul,* both sure
and stedfast, and which entereth into that within the veil.
                               —Hebrews 6:17–19 (emphasis added)

Questions to Consider

1. Have your ever tried to put yourself in the situations of people
   like Noah and Jonah? Noah preached for 120 years about
   coming destruction, yet his only converts were the members
   of his family. Would you have that kind of tenacity? Jonah
   entered a city that was known for its absolutely barbaric ways.
   Today, it is difficult to find Christians who will pass out tracts
   in inner-city sections of large metropolitan areas, yet we criticize Jonah for his initial lack of faith. Are we any different
   from him?
2. During basic training in the U.S. Navy during World War II,
   sailors were taught a vital survival lesson: If the ship they were
   on should ever be torpedoed and start to sink, the sailors should
   try to row or swim as far away from it as possible. This was
   because a sinking ship creates a swirling vortex that will pull
   everything down with it. Have you known people or businesses
   or groups that were like that: as they sank further and further
   into sin they pulled everything down with them? Beware of such
   whirlpools of disaster.
3. The *Titanic* was called "the ship even God couldn't sink," yet on
   its first voyage it hit an iceberg and sank. Did it ever occur to
   you that while man was making the *Titanic,* God was making
   the iceberg?

SUGGESTED ADDITIONAL READINGS

Fruchtenbaum, Arnold G. *The Footsteps of the Messiah.* Tustin, Calif.:
   Ariel Press, 1982.

Houghton, S. M. *Sketches from Church History*. Carlisle, Pa.: Banner of
    Truth Trust, 1980.
Lewis, J. M. *How's Your Family?* New York: Brunner/Mazel, 1989.
McMinn, Don. *Strategic Living*. Grand Rapids: Baker, 1983.
Thurman, Chris. *The Twelve Best Kept Secrets for Living an Emotion-
    ally Healthy Life*. Nashville: Nelson, 1993.

CHAPTER 12

THE SCENT OF DEATH

Have you ever smelled something that instantly triggered a memory? The whiff of a certain perfume might bring back memories of your first date. The aroma of baked turkey might make you recall a special Thanksgiving dinner at your grandmother's house. The scent of shoe polish might generate memories of your first week at boot camp.

I'm sure we've all experienced times when a fragrance, an odor, or a scent of something has instantly made us recall some specific experience in life.

For me, that occurs whenever I smell formaldehyde. The pungent, tart odor of formaldehyde always makes me think of death. I cannot separate the two. That's because the first time I ever smelled formaldehyde, I was in a high school biology class where for a year we students dissected flatworms, frogs, and a small pig. Each specimen was very dead, and each had come sealed in a jar of formaldehyde.

I hated that smell. I still do. Cutting into formerly living creatures—even for the cause of science—was never something I liked to do. Even today, when I walk by the science halls at the university where I teach, I don't go near the laboratories. I just don't want to be near the scent of death.

I've discovered I'm not alone in this. In Jack London's best-known short story, "To Build a Fire," London gives an example of the fear and aversion all living creatures have for the scent of death. At the story's end, a foolish traveler who has gotten his feet wet freezes to death because he has gone traveling alone when it is seventy degrees below zero. The man now sits rigid on the ground. His dog cannot figure out why the man won't walk, or at least build a fire.

London writes, "The man remained silent. Later, the dog whined loudly. And still later it crept close to the man and caught the scent of death. This made the animal bristle and back away."

This small scene grips the reader, for anyone who has ever been confronted by the scent of death is able to relate to the dog's reaction. It's almost as though we feel that if we are close enough to smell death, we may also be close enough for it to "catch" us. We recoil immediately and back away.

Because the scent of death is so horrifying, the Bible tells us that learning how to transcend death is like inhaling a fragrant bouquet. Accepting Christ as one's personal Savior changes the stench of death into the aroma of roses. Formaldehyde becomes perfume.

As representatives and witnesses of Christ, we are able to convey His appealing fragrance of everlasting life to everyone we meet. The apostle Paul wrote in 2 Corinthians 2:14–15, "But thanks be to God, who always leads us in His triumph in Christ, and manifests through us the sweet aroma of the knowledge of Him in every place. For we are a fragrance of Christ to God among those who are being saved and among those who are perishing" (NASB).

As a person who has made hospital visits to people who are entering the final phase of a terminal illness, I can say that people have a keen awareness of when the scent of death is descending on them.

For those who are secure in the salvation of Christ, it is like the warmly recognizable aroma of being home; it has the familiar smells of a very comfortable setting. People welcome this and are relaxed by it.

But for those who are outside of God's grace, the scent of death is a putrid and threatening stench. It causes people to bristle and whine just like the dog in Jack London's short story. They want to escape, but there is no escape. The apostle Paul explained that these people know that they are going from the death of physical life to the death of eternal damnation (2 Cor. 2:16). It's a horrifying realization.

If we really care about saving lost souls, we need to start putting our noses into other people's business. We need to find out what people's spiritual lives smell like. Do we recognize the sweet aroma of a redeemed life or do we detect the dry rot of sin? Trust your instinct: the nose knows.

The Egyptians used to embalm bodies with cloves, myrrh, spices, and incense as a way of counteracting the smell of decaying flesh. None of it endured. The scent of death was too overwhelming. Without the "fragrance of Christ," people are, at best, merely decaying flesh.

And not even formaldehyde can change that.

THINKING MORE ABOUT CHAPTER 12

Scripture Verses to Ponder

> Then took Mary a pound of ointment of spikenard, very costly, and anointed the feet of Jesus, and wiped his feet with her hair: and the house was filled with the odour of the ointment. Then saith one of his disciples, Judas Iscariot, Simon's son, which should betray him, Why was not this ointment sold for three hundred pence, and given to the poor? This he said, not that he cared for the poor; but because he was a thief, and had the bag, and bare what was put therein. Then said Jesus, Let her alone: against the day of my burying hath she kept this. For the poor always ye have with you; but me ye have not always.
>
> —John 12:3–8

> But I have all, and abound: I am full, having received of Epaphroditus the things which were sent from you, an odour of a sweet smell, a sacrifice acceptable, well-pleasing to God.
>
> —Philippians 4:18

And when he had taken the book, the four beasts and four and twenty elders fell down before the Lamb, having every one of them harps, and golden vials full of odours, which are the prayers of saints.

—Revelation 5:8

Questions to Consider

1. Isn't it amazing how God has created your sensory powers to work together to assist each other? If the smoke alarm should go off in your house in the middle of the night, the ears will hear the alarm, the nose will smell the smoke, the fingers will feel for the telephone in the darkened room. Everything works together to protect you. God's creation of the human body is a continuous source of blessing and wonderment.

2. Animals have an extraordinary sense of smell. Dogs can be trained to follow trails, detect drugs within luggage, and find lost children. But dogs have no reasoning power. Men and women, however, who do not have so keen a sense of smell, have the ability to discern the significance of various fragrances and odors. Have you ever considered what a wonderful deciphering system God built into your brain? Truly, we are "fearfully and wonderfully made" (Ps. 139:14).

3. In Old Testament times the saints of God offered burnt offerings as a tribute to God. In Revelation, however, we are told that our prayers are like perfume to God. What messages are you wafting to God this week—the scent of charred animal flesh or the sweet fragrance of prayer?

4. Could your personal testimony be ruined by the smells coming from you? Is there a whiff of alcohol on your breath, a scent of tobacco smoke in your clothes? There shouldn't be! Be careful. Use good sense in order to maintain good scents.

Suggested Additional Readings

Bonhoeffer, Dietrich. *Life Together.* New York: Harper and Row, 1952.

Ferguson, David and Teresa, and Chris and Holly Thurman. *The Pursuit of Intimacy.* Nashville: Nelson, 1993.

Kelly, Thomas R. *A Testament of Devotion.* New York: Harper and Brothers, 1941.

Laubach, Frank C. *Prayer Is the Mightiest Force in the World.* New York: Revell, 1946.

Wallis, Arthus. *God's Chosen Fast.* Fort Washington, Pa.: Christian Literature Crusade, 1969.

CHAPTER 13

WAVING FROM THE SHORES

A few years ago, I was asked to come to a rest home to be at the bedside of an elderly man who was near death. In my work as a church deacon, I had visited Mr. Barkoviak many times before; so, knowing his time was near, he sent for me.

"I wanted you to know why I don't regret dying," he said to me, his frail hand resting on my arm. I leaned forward to hear him better.

"I came to America from Poland in 1919," he explained. "My parents sold the family cow and all of our chickens to help pay my passage. They knew, in all likelihood, they would never see me again once I left. But there was no future for me in Poland. And several of my cousins and some of our village neighbors had already gone to America. They promised to help me get situated once I arrived."

I nodded, encouraging him to continue.

"I rode in the back of a wagon as I left our village. My heart was breaking. My mother and father and my little sister were waving to me. My neighbors and one of my schoolteachers and even my childhood sweetheart were all there, waving continually until I was too far away to see them any longer.

"The trip was harsh. From a wagon to a boxcar on a train to the lowest storage deck of a filthy freighter, I traveled for five weeks. I was always hungry, often wet and cold, and continually lonely. I cried many times and wished desperately that I could go back home.

"At long last our freighter arrived in New York harbor and I saw the Statue of Liberty. I was awed by it. After processing through Ellis Island, I left a small brick building. There, some fifty yards away, yet visible, was a group of people from my village. They were shouting my name and waving their arms and calling words of welcome in Polish.

"I could see my favorite cousin, Edju, whom I had climbed trees with as a boy. And Mr. Kolat, our blacksmith, was there. He was still big and burly. And Mrs. Dukowski, the only redhead in our village, was near the front holding a freshly baked pie for me. Many, many others were there, too. And all were waving and calling to me.

"I broke into a run, waving back to them. My heart was pounding and my eyes were filled with tears of joy. I showed my clearance papers to the final guard, then pushed through the gates of the last clearing fence and rushed into the open arms of my friends. We hugged and laughed and cried and were ecstatically happy to see each other again.

"I had food pressed on me by all the women, and I ate ravenously. Everyone seemed to be talking at once. How was my trip? What news could I share from my village? How were my parents? Did I have messages from anyone else's relatives? Everyone was terribly delighted to see me, and I was overjoyed to be met and welcomed this way. It was the happiest moment of my life. I was back with all my friends."

He paused a moment in thought.

"And that's why I don't regret dying," he said at last. "I wanted you here so that I could wave good-bye. I'm sorry to have to leave you, but a new place beckons to me. When there was nothing left for me in Poland, I moved to America. Now, there's nothing left for me on this earth, so I'm moving again. And I'm happy about that. There are a lot of people waving to me, ready to welcome me to that new shore. But this time it won't be Mrs. Dukowski who'll be out front, it'll be my Savior. And that'll make this even more wonderful than the last time."

He then closed his eyes and tried to relax a bit, tired from the exhaustion of talking. I pulled a chair near his bed.

"I'll sit here and wave until you're out of sight," I told him.

He smiled gently, his eyes still closed.

"And I'll wave to you from the other side," he promised, "when it comes time for you to start the trip."

THINKING MORE ABOUT CHAPTER 13

Scripture Verses to Ponder

> I will give you the keys of the kingdom of heaven; whatever you bind on earth will be bound in heaven, and whatever you loose on earth will be loosed in heaven.
>
> —Matthew 16:19 (NIV)

> Nothing will harm you. However, do not rejoice that the spirits submit to you, but rejoice that your names are written in heaven.
>
> —Luke 10:19–20 (NIV)

> But our citizenship is in heaven. And we eagerly await a Savior from there, the Lord Jesus Christ, who, by the power that enables him to bring everything under his control, will transform our lowly bodies so that they will be like his glorious body.
>
> —Philippians 3:20–21 (NIV)

> The Lord will rescue me from every evil attack and will bring me safely to his heavenly kingdom. To him be glory for ever and ever. Amen.
>
> —2 Timothy 4:18 (NIV)

Questions to Consider

1. Regarding the death of a Christian, the apostle Paul wrote, "Brothers, we do not want you to be ignorant about those who fall asleep, or to grieve like the rest of men, who have no hope. We believe that Jesus died and rose again and so we believe that God will bring with Jesus those who have fallen asleep in him" (1 Thess. 4:13–14 NIV) How is this comforting to people who have lost children or siblings or parents? How do these words make us feel when at a funeral for a friend?

2. Many popular gospel tunes use such phrases as "when the saints go marching in" and "we shall meet on that beautiful shore" and "when we all get to heaven, what a day of rejoicing that will be." In what ways do you think fellowship will be similar to the way it was on earth, and in what ways do you think it will be different?

3. Sometimes when people are spending a week of vacation at the beach or are relaxing in a whirlpool at a spa, they will remark, "Ahhh, this is heaven." Why is that a ridiculous statement?

4. Does knowing that you will see your Christian friends and loved ones in heaven one day have an effect on how you treat them currently here on earth?

SUGGESTED ADDITIONAL READINGS

Brandt, Henry R. *The Struggle for Peace.* Wheaton, Ill.: Scripture Press, 1965.

Bright, Bill. *The Holy Spirit.* San Bernardino, Calif.: Here's Life, 1980.

Christensen, Evelyn. *"Lord, Change Me!"* Wheaton, Ill.: Victor Books, 1977.

Cook, William H. *Success, Motivation and the Scriptures.* Nashville: Broadman-Holman, 1974.

Kaiser, Walter C. *A Biblical Approach to Personal Suffering.* Chicago: Moody, 1982.

CHAPTER 14

THE VOICE OF GOD

Have you ever stopped to think about the range of power there is in the voice of God?

Usually, we dwell primarily on the creative power of God's voice. Genesis 1 tells us, "God said, Let there be light . . . firmament . . . waters . . . grass . . . the herb yielding seed and the fruit tree . . . and it was so." God *spoke* the world into existence. How marvelous!

What we also need to remember, however, is that this same voice has the power to reverse the creative process and to bring judgment upon evil mankind. God has done it before with a great flood, fire from heaven, storms, and drought; and in the future He will do it again with earthquakes, lightning, thunder, and hail (Rev. 8:5–7).

Although God's power is incomprehensible, we can get a glimpse of His might if we relate passages of Scripture to events of tangible measurement.

The psalmist tells us, "He [God] uttered his voice, the earth melted" (Ps. 46:6). What sort of power does it take to melt the earth? Let's consider for a moment the volcanic eruption of Mount St. Helens on May 18, 1980, in the state of Washington.

According to *Geology* magazine (vol. 11) and *Scientific American* (vol. 244, no. 3), the steam-based energy output from Mount St. Helens on May 18 was equivalent to 400 million tons of dynamite (which is *20,000 times* more powerful than the atomic bomb dropped on Hiroshima). The eruption flattened about one hundred fifty square miles of timber (four billion board feet, enough to build about three hundred thousand two-bedroom homes) and expelled 1.4 billion cubic yards of pulverized rock in the form of ash.

In the aftermath of the May 18 eruption, mud slides of dirt and lava gouged out a 140-feet deep canyon at the headwaters of the Toutle River Valley. More than 600 feet of layered ash, lava, soot, mud, and volcanic debris fell back to earth after the eruption. Approximately nineteen thousand tree stumps were blown into nearby Spirit Lake by volcanic steam blasts.

This sort of power is mind-boggling, yet in scientific circles the Mount St. Helens eruption is considered a "small" volcanic event. In August 1883, a volcano erupted on the island of Krakatoa in Indonesia. It was so powerful, it destroyed everything on the island *and* created a tidal wave so huge, it killed thirty-six thousand people as far away as Java and Sumatra. Airborne debris from the volcano was blown all the way from Southeast Asia clear across the Indian Ocean to the island of Madagascar, off the east coast of Africa.

In A.D. 79, Mount Vesuvius in southern Italy erupted and completely buried the two metropolitan areas of Herculaneum and Pompeii in lava and ash. Its explosion happened so fast that, eighteen hundred years later, bodies were found still perfectly encased in rock. This volcano erupted again in 1906, 1929, and 1944 and is still considered to be active today.

These three examples make it apparent that "melting" the earth requires power and energy of a phenomenal magnitude. Yet, God has only to speak in order to accomplish this. It is no wonder then that His voice has been feared and revered throughout the ages. When the Jews were told that Moses had heard the voice of God in the burning bush, they were absolutely amazed to learn that hearing such an awesome voice had not immediately killed Moses (Deut. 4:33). Even God Himself once described His voice as having the power of thunder (Job 40:9).

Truly, it would be terrifying to have to worry about trying to withstand the voice of God if it were turned against us. But as yet, it has not been. Instead, through Christ, the voice of God is one of gentle urging. Jesus has promised, "If any man hear my voice, and open the door, I will come in to him" (Rev. 3:20). Jesus is beckoning all people to accept His shed blood as the atonement for their sins and to be redeemed and saved by His righteousness.

Those who turn a deaf ear to the voice of God now will not elude Him forever. When He returns, He will do so "with a shout" (1 Thess. 4:16) and, just like the flash of a volcano's eruption, His shout will bring "sudden destruction" (5:3) on all who previously ignored His voice.

I hope you're listening.

THINKING MORE ABOUT CHAPTER 14

Scripture Verses to Ponder

> Did ever people hear the voice of God speaking out of the midst of the fire, as thou hast heard, and live?
>
> —Deuteronomy 4:33

> Hast thou an arm like God? or canst thou thunder with a voice like him?
>
> —Job 40:9

> The Lord also thundered in the heavens, and the Highest gave his voice; hail stones and coals of fire.
>
> —Psalm 18:13

> And the Lord shall utter his voice before his army: for his camp is very great: for he is strong that executeth his word: for the day of the Lord is great and very terrible; and who can abide it?
>
> —Joel 2:11

For the Lord himself shall descend from heaven with a shout,
with the voice of the archangel, and with the trump of God:
and the dead in Christ shall rise first.

—1 Thessalonians 4:16

Questions to Consider

1. Although you have never had a burning bush talk to you, were
   there times in your life when you felt God was speaking to your
   heart and mind? What were those circumstances? How did you
   respond to this leading and what were the results?
2. An old hymn reminds us, "Jesus is tenderly calling today." Have
   you ever taken time to consider all the different reasons Jesus is
   calling us? He is calling us from a world of sin. He is calling us
   to service. What other reasons can you think of that causes Jesus
   to call us?
3. For many decades the emblem of the Radio Corporation of
   America (RCA) has been a dog with its ear inclined toward the
   playing horn of an old-fashioned wind-up phonograph. Beneath
   the dog's photo are the words, "His master's voice." Could this
   be said of you, too? Do you go through your day with your ear
   inclined toward your Master's voice?
4. A lion tamer once explained to an audience that the wild tigers
   and lions who obey his command do so because they discern
   the power of the lion tamer's voice. Someone else could stand
   in the cage and say the same words, yet the animals would not
   obey. How about you? Can you discern the voice of the One
   who controls your life? Can you recognize what is the voice of
   Satan and what is the voice of God? If not, you'd better spend
   some more time in God's Holy Word so that you'll know who's
   talking to you.

SUGGESTED ADDITIONAL READINGS

Cox, Harvey. *The Feast of Fools.* Cambridge: Harvard University Press, 1969.

Erickson, Millard J. *Truth or Consequences.* Downers Grove, Ill.: NavPress, 2001.

Glist, Virginia J. *Lend an Ear.* Indianapolis: R & R Newkirk Co., 1983.

Laubach, Frank C. *Learning the Vocabulary of God.* Nashville: Upper Room, 1956.

Law, William. *A Serious Call to a Devout and Holy Life.* Nashville: Upper Room, 1952.

Nichols, R., and L. A. Stevens. *Are You Listening?* New York: McGraw-Hill, 1957.

CHAPTER 15

THE ORIGINAL "BLOOD, SWEAT, AND TEARS" SPEECH

At a point of low morale in England during World War II, Prime Minister Winston Churchill gave a rousing radio address in which he doggedly insisted, "We shall *never* surrender!"

In great candor, Churchill did not promise the British people that he would find an easy way for them to win the war. Quite the contrary. He warned that to lead them to victory he would demand of them their "blood, sweat, toil, and tears." But because the British people were willing to make these painful sacrifices, they ultimately were victorious.

Interestingly enough, 1,880 years before Churchill gave his now famous address, the apostle Paul gave his own "blood, sweat, and tears" speech. Paul's listeners were the leaders of the Christian churches at Ephesus. Unlike Churchill, however, who demanded sacrifices *from* the people, Paul explained that blood, sweat, and tears had been given *to* the people.

And just as the words of Churchill can yet impress free people everywhere to sacrifice everything in order to maintain their *political* liberties, so, too, can the words of the apostle Paul inspire Christians everywhere to appreciate the great sacrifices that have been made to secure their *spiritual* liberties.

THE BLOOD

In Acts 20:28 Paul reminded the Ephesian pastors that they were obligated to care for their congregations with the greatest of diligence. This obligation came from the fact that the church had been redeemed by Christ "with his own blood." If Jesus had been willing to show that degree of care, surely these pastors must not belittle this sacrifice by failing to share His love with as many people as possible.

Paul, himself, measured up to this responsibility. As a teacher and evangelist he reminded them, "I . . . have taught you . . . from house to house, Testifying both to the Jews, and also to the Greeks, . . . faith toward our Lord Jesus Christ" (Acts 20:20–21).

To this end, no man could spend eternity in hell and blame Paul for never having shared the gospel with him. Paul proclaimed, "I am pure from the blood of all men" (Acts 20:26). He was guiltless on that account.

So it was then that Paul admonished the Ephesians to be washed in the righteous blood of Christ but to be free of the guilty blood of lost men.

THE SWEAT

Although Paul's calling from God was to evangelize the Gentiles, Paul never considered himself better than any other man. To put action to this belief, Paul performed manual labor, usually as a tent maker, to support himself and those who traveled with him. He explained to the Ephesians that he did this hard work to teach them by example how they should not be a burden to others, but, instead, should be helpers to the weaker and less fortunate people around them. As Paul explained his actions, "These hands have ministered unto my necessities, *and* to them that were with me" (Acts 20:34, emphasis added).

When Adam fell from grace, God's judgment was, "In the sweat of thy face shalt thou eat bread" (Gen. 3:19). The apostle Paul showed that no Christian—himself included—was exempt from this admonition. Honest, hard work never goes out of vogue.

THE TEARS

Paul's heart was so broken for lost souls, he literally mourned over people who resisted his call to salvation. Paul asked for no earthly gold, silver, or fine clothing. He sought only the redemption of sinners. As he explained to the Ephesians, he had "serv[ed] the Lord with all humility of mind, and with many tears" (Acts 20:19).

Paul's yearning to reach the lost with the love of Christ was so sincere, he worked day and night, year after year, with pleading tears, imploring people to be saved. "By the space of three years," Paul reminded them, "I ceased not to warn every one night and day with tears" (Acts 20:31).

Whereas it might be easy to reject the approaches of fast-talking salesmen or the false flattery of an insincere friend, it is almost impossible not to be touched deeply by the tears of genuine concern someone sheds for us. Paul truly ached over the condition of wayward souls. He did all he could to show compassion for them. And whereas he shed tears of concern over those who were lost, like the father of the prodigal son (Luke 15:20), he also shed tears of joy over each soul that was found. Tears of anguish, tears of joy. Paul knew them both.

THE VICTORY

Winston Churchill gave his "blood, sweat, and tears" speech on May 13, 1940. Five years later, on May 8, 1945 (V-E Day), the British people finally achieved their victory over their Nazi aggressors. During those five bitter years, tens of thousands of British citizens were killed or maimed, families lost loved ones, and tears flowed unceasingly. The awesome price paid by the British people for freedom from tyranny has never been forgotten.

The apostle Paul gave his "blood, sweat, and tears" speech in A.D. 60. He spoke of a victory, through Christ, that had already been won. The tyranny of sin had been subdued by the power of Christ's blood. The irony here was that the victims of this great war were not those who had fought the battle but only those who failed to acknowledge that the victory had actually been achieved. For them, the blood had been shed; but, because they wouldn't accept it, tears continued to flow unceasingly.

Those tears continue to flow today. Churchill's speech was a call to battle. The apostle Paul's speech was an announcement of victory. In both situations the blood, the sweat, and the tears were prevalent. How we perceive them—as things to be demanded *from* people or as things that have been sacrificed *for* people—is what will make all the difference.

THINKING MORE ABOUT CHAPTER 15

Scripture Verses to Ponder

In the sweat of thy face shalt thou eat bread, till thou return unto the ground; for out of it wast thou taken: for dust thou art, and unto dust shalt thou return.

—Genesis 3:19

Serving the Lord with all humility of mind, and with many tears, and temptations, which befell me by the lying in wait of the Jews.

—Acts 20:19

Wherefore I take you to record this day, that I am pure from the blood of all men.

—Acts 20:26

Take heed therefore unto yourselves, and to all the flock, over the which the Holy Ghost hath made you overseers, to feed the church of God, which he hath purchased with his own blood.

—Acts 20:28

Therefore watch, and remember, that by the space of three years I ceased not to warn every one night and day with tears.

—Acts 20:31

Questions to Consider

1. Have you ever thought about the different levels of intensity of service between Christ and His disciples? While Jesus prayed so fervently in the garden that blood and sweat mingled on His forehead, the disciples were lying down sound asleep. How fervent is your service to God? Are you vibrantly intense . . . or lying down on the job?

2. If you have ever been a blood donor, you know that the first thing the nurse does is take one drop of blood from your finger. She puts it into a vial of solution to see if it has enough iron in it to sink to the bottom. Blood that is too anemic, too thin, or too undernourished is of no use to someone else. How strong do you feel the blood of Christ is, to be of use to you? Do you trust it to cleanse your sins and make you righteous before God?

3. How intense are the tears you shed for lost souls? Many years ago a farmer witnessed each week to the blacksmith of his town, trying to convert him to Christianity. The blacksmith refused to yield. The farmer quoted Scripture, shared Bible stories, and told of the miracles of Christ, but still the blacksmith would not

surrender his heart to Jesus. Finally, one Sunday morning the farmer came to the blacksmith to beg him to go to church with him; however, when he thought of his friend the blacksmith dying and going to hell, the farmer could not talk. He just stood and cried. This caused the blacksmith to yield.

SUGGESTED ADDITIONAL READINGS

Benner, David. *Healing Emotional Wounds.* Grand Rapids: Baker, 1990.

Boise, James Montgomery. *Whatever Happened to the Gospel of Grace?* Wheaton, Ill.: Crossway Books, 2000.

Getz, Gene. *Loving One Another.* Wheaton, Ill.: Victor Books, 1980.

Halliday, Steve. *Faith Is Stranger Than Fiction.* Green Forest, Ark.: New Leaf Press, 2000.

Rohm, Robert A. *Positive Personality Profiles.* Atlanta: Personality Insights, 1993.

Steere, Douglas. *Prayer and Worship.* New York: Edward Hazen Foundation, 1942.

Swindoll, Charles. *The Grace Awakening.* Dallas: Word, 1990.

CHAPTER 16

WHAT'S COOKING?

Our fathers . . . ate the same spiritual food; and all drank the
same spiritual drink, for they were drinking from a spiritual
rock which followed them; and the rock was Christ.
—1 Corinthians 10:1–4 (NASB)

Both of my grandmothers were excellent southern cooks from Tennessee. They used to make scratch biscuits every morning. These biscuits were always golden brown, light, fluffy, warm, and absolutely
delicious.

The fact that they tasted so good was a continual mystery to me
when I was a boy because the individual ingredients seemed so unpal-
atable. I tasted the lard used for greasing the pan—yuck! I tasted the
flour—bland! I tasted the yeast—gritty! I tasted the salt—bitter! I tasted
the water—flat! I tasted the baking soda—tart!

There was no taste appeal to any one of those ingredients; yet, when
combined into dough and then baked, they created very tasty biscuits.

I think the life of a Christian is sometimes analyzed this same way.
People look at its individual components—its "ingredients"—rather
than at its finished product. From an outsider's viewpoint, the

stewardship, discipline, belief, faithfulness, and spirituality aspects of the Christian life may seem to be too rigid and too limiting to allow for much enjoyment in life. However, just the opposite is true.

As a deacon and counselor, I've been asked on numerous occasions to try to offer some sort of emotional comfort and encouragement to parents whose children have been hurt or killed as a result of drunk driving or use of drugs.

Often these parents will say, "Our son used to laugh at the Christian kids in his school. He called them squares and oddballs because they wouldn't attend the wild parties on the weekends. Now, those young people are getting ready to leave for college next fall, and our son is dead. Those other kids have fabulous lives and careers ahead of them, but our boy is gone. He told us he just wanted to have a little fun. I wish he could have been more like them."

Similarly, I've spent time talking to elderly people in rest homes. On more than one occasion I've had someone tell me, "I made a fortune in my life and spent most of it on myself. Now that I'm old, no one comes to see me. I never really invested myself or my money in anyone else. There's a fellow across the hall, however, who hardly made a dime all his life, yet he has people dropping in continually. He used to teach Sunday school and his students still check up on him. Even more amazing, when he's alone, he can take out his Bible and sit there for hours enjoying himself. I used to call people like that 'fools.' Now I wish I had what he has."

What non-Christians don't understand is that each part of the Christian walk enhances the other. In the biscuit recipe, the water allowed the other ingredients to blend as one, the yeast enabled the dough to rise, the baking soda aerated the mixture, and so on.

Likewise, in the Christian walk, the faithfulness of church attendance and Bible study undergirds feelings of personal spirituality; the discipline of abstaining from substances that may harm the body provides protection from injury or disease; the practice of stewardship allows a sense of sharing, helping and cooperating to develop within the individual and, thus, enhance discipline (with money) and faith (in God's care and in the concern of other believers). One spiritual "ingredient" brings out the best of what the other ingredients have to offer: they combine to offer a main course of Christian living.

When I was a boy, I always looked forward to starting the day by filling myself with those delicious biscuits made from all those different ingredients. Today, I look forward to starting each day by filling myself with the spirituality of Christ, which also is made from many different ingredients.

THINKING MORE ABOUT CHAPTER 16

Scripture Verses to Ponder

> But solid food is for the mature, who by constant use have trained themselves to distinguish good from evil.
> —Hebrews 5:14 (NIV)

> Like newborn babies, crave pure spiritual milk, so that by it you may grow up in your salvation, now that you have tasted that the Lord is good.
> —1 Peter 2:2–3 (NIV)

Questions to Consider

1. Have you ever thought of your life as being a recipe of all the "ingredients" you pour into it? Take a moment and make notes about what all you are "mixing" into your life:
   - In what ways are you adding joy?
   - In what ways are you adding service to Christ?
   - In what ways are you adding Bible study?
   - In what ways are you adding service to your local church?
2. If you leave out even one ingredient in a recipe for biscuits, the recipe won't work. You *must* have flour, you *must* have baking soda, you *must* have water, and so on. Have you ever tried to

leave certain ingredients out of your Christian life: tithing? church attendance? witnessing? If so, what sort of end product did you end up with? What did you learn from that experience?

SUGGESTED ADDITIONAL READINGS

Berkhof, Louis. *Systematic Theology.* Grand Rapids: Eerdmans, 1941.

Carter, Les. *Broken Vows.* Nashville: Nelson, 1990.

Heitzig, Skip. *Jesus Up Close.* Wheaton, Ill.: Tyndale House, 2000.

Horn, Robert M. *Go Free.* Downers Grove, Ill.: InterVarsity, 1976.

Murray, John. *Redemption: Accomplished and Applied.* Grand Rapids: Eerdmans, 1965.

Pink, Arthur W. *Present-Day Evangelism.* Swengel, Pa.: Bible Truth Depot, n.d.

Pritchard, Ray. *In the Shadow of the Cross.* Nashville: Broadman-Holman, 2000.

CHAPTER 17

IT'S ALWAYS NEW YEAR'S EVE FOR A CHRISTIAN

Not long ago my wife and I were attending a New Year's Eve get-together with friends. The hostess was passing out party hats and noise-makers, getting ready to ring in the new year, when a man next to me gave out a heavy sigh and slumped into a chair.

"I hope this next year will be better for me than this last one has been," the man said, his head lowered. "This has been one of the worst years of my life. I lost money in the stock market, my pet collie died, I broke my arm while playing softball, my wife wrecked our family car in an accident, and my son flunked out of college and moved back in with us. Man, what a year! Thank goodness it's New Year's Eve. Now I've got a chance to start fresh again."

I completely understood the man's desire to start anew, what with all the unfortunate things that had been happening to him. What I couldn't understand, however, was why he felt he had to wait until January 1 in order to get at it.

As Christians, we serve a God who tells us, "Behold, I make all things new" (Rev. 21:5). No matter how bad things may be for us today, with Jesus we can start things anew tomorrow. He can forgive our sins, put our weaknesses behind us, and blot out our failures. The Bible prom-ises us that "the LORD's mercies . . . are new every morning" (Lam. 3:22–23). Every dawn can signal another New Year's Day for a Chris-tian. There's no reason Christians shouldn't start a new life with each new day.

Just think of how each month already provides some sort of new beginning. March, June, September, and December are all months that start new seasons. High school graduates begin a new life after gradu-ation in May. Brides and grooms begin a new life when they have June weddings. In late August a new school year begins. Various sports be-gin their seasons in a wide variety of months. The calendar is full of first months, first weeks, first days.

In a similar way, the Bible teaches us that we can be continually new. We became something fresh and new the very moment we ac-cepted Christ as our Savior. Second Corinthians 5:17 explains, "There-fore if any man be in Christ, he is a new creature: old things are passed away; behold, all things are become new." When we came to Jesus, we shed our old ways and former sin.

But *who*, you may ask, is this "new creature"? The Bible tells us that when Christ established His church, He created a new person to popu-late it: *the Christian*. He eliminated Jews and Gentiles so that this "one new man" (Eph. 2:15) would stand mutually equal in God's kingdom. You are a child of the king, an heir to His heavenly realm, an alien on earth waiting to be called to your true home. Indeed, you are some-thing new.

Everything about you is new. Upon becoming a Christian you were given "newness of life" (Rom. 6:4), as well as "newness of spirit" (7:6).

Your new life as a Christian has given you new power, too. You need no animal sacrifices or chants of a priest in order to call on God. You are able "to enter into the holiest [presence of God] by the blood of Jesus, By a *new* and living way, which he hath consecrated for us, through the veil, that is to say, his flesh" (Heb. 10:19–20, emphasis added).

It is though this "new and living way" that we can "die daily" to sin and start afresh with new enthusiasm and new goals. The blood of

Jesus cleanses us and makes us new; it empowers us with the ability to come daily into His presence to seek forgiveness whenever we falter; it continually gives us a fresh start in life.

Consider for a moment how much you enjoy turning over the page of a new month on a calendar. You see new squares without notes or scribbles. The page is clean. It feels good to tear off the old month and discard it. It's behind you now. So, too, can our "old ways" be put behind us when we begin anew with God.

Let today be New Year's Eve for you. Go to God in prayer. Confess your sins. Ask forgiveness. Accept forgiveness. Put your burdens before God and seek His guidance and wisdom. Open your heart to His leading. Spend time in Bible study. Trust God for new strength and new encouragement.

Having done all this, smile. Celebrate. This is a joyous occasion. Your life is now starting with a clean slate.

Happy New Year, brother!

THINKING MORE ABOUT CHAPTER 17

Scripture Verses to Ponder

Are thy days as the days of man? are thy years as man's days?
—Job 10:5

Thou crownest the year with thy goodness. . . .
—Psalm 65:11

Preach the acceptable year of the Lord.
—Luke 4:19

Having therefore, brethren, boldness to enter into the holiest by the blood of Jesus, By a *new* and living way, which he hath consecrated for us, through the veil, that is to say, his flesh.
—Hebrews 10:19–20 (emphasis added)

Him that overcometh will I make a pillar in the temple of my
God, and he shall go no more out: and I will write upon him
the name of my God, and the name of the city of my God,
which is new Jerusalem, which cometh down out of heaven
from my God: and I will write upon him my *new* name.

—Revelation 3:12 (emphasis added)

Questions to Consider

1. Imagine that you are going to make tomorrow a New Year's beginning for yourself. What are six New Year's resolutions you
   feel would improve your walk with God and your relationship
   with other people?

   A.

   B.

   C.

   D.

   E.

   F.

2. Think about the seasons of the year. What makes a crisp autumn day so invigorating? What makes spring feel like the world
   is full of great potential? Are there ways that you can keep the
   crispness of autumn and the freshness of spring inside you all
   year long?

3. If you could relive any year of your life, which year would it be?
   What was so special about that year? Are there lessons or ideas
   from that "great" year that you can apply to the year you are
   now living in?

4. We divide our historical past into two sections: the years "before Christ" lived on Earth (B.C.) and the "anno domini" or years since His birth (A.D.). How was your life different during the years before you accepted Christ as your Savior?

SUGGESTED ADDITIONAL READINGS

Bennett, Arnold. *How to Live on 24 Hours a Day.* New York: Cornerstone Library, 1962.

Engstrom, Ted W., and Alex R. MacKenzie. *Managing Your Time: Practical Guidelines on the Effective Use of Time.* Grand Rapids: Zondervan, 1967.

Hensley, Dennis E. *How to Manage Your Time: Time Management Strategies for Active Christians.* Anderson, Ind.: Warner Press, 1989.

———. *Millennium Approaches.* New York: Avon, 1998.

Hinson, Ed, and Lee Fredrickson. *Future Wave.* Eugene, Ore.: Harvest House, 2000.

McKenzie, R. Alex. *The Time Trap.* New York: AMACON, 1972.

Webber, Ross A. *Time and Management.* New York: Van Nostrand Reinhold Co., 1972.

CHAPTER 18

GODLY GUMPTION OVERCOMES SHYNESS

Have you ever "postponed" an opportunity to witness to someone about the saving grace of Jesus Christ because you felt shy and self-conscious? Maybe it's time you learned how to overcome this outreach barrier.

Shyness isn't something we've just discovered in recent years. People have suffered from it since ancient times—partly because the problem was so often ignored or passed off lightly.

"What? Shy? *My* wife? Naw, she's just a little moody, that's all."

"Yeah, I know my boy's bashful. No big deal. The kid'll come out of his shell when he gets a little older."

"My daughter is shy, eh? So? Who cares? Little girls are supposed to be coy, right?"

Those responses are naive. The truth is that words such as *shyness* and *bashfulness* are just a cover for the real problem: *Fear.* Experts agree that shy people are genuinely afraid of something.

Their fears can be real or imagined. And the sad irony is that Christians are often among the shyest of people. They can read Scripture passages about walking through the valley of the shadow of death and fearing no evil, yet refuse to go out on calling night because they are terrified of having to meet strangers.

Too often, our fears become stronger than our faith, and we miss opportunities to receive spiritual gifts from God. When God called Moses to speak to Pharaoh, Moses complained that he was not eloquent enough to handle the job. His complaining angered the Lord (Exod. 4:14).

"I will be thy mouth, . . . and will teach you what ye shall do," God promised Moses (v. 15). But Moses lacked confidence. As a result, his brother, Aaron, became God's spokesman. Moses had a chance to receive the gift of spiritually inspired oratory (1 Cor. 12:8), but his shyness and fear made him forfeit this blessing.

Religious and lay counselors agree that shyness hasn't been taken seriously enough. It can become an excuse for a lack of assertiveness in men with poor work records, both in their church and secular jobs. But it can be dealt with if men truly have a desire to overcome it.

"When it comes to overcoming shyness, everything comes down to attitude and preparation," says Dr. L. Stanley Wenck, a professor of psychology at Ball State University. "Men who *anticipate* that they are going to behave awkwardly around other people are actually *programming* themselves to behave that way. Instead, they should develop an attitude of confidence."

Dr. Wenck works with college freshmen who are living away from home for the first time and are feeling shy because of their new surroundings. The tips he gives these young adults are also useful to any Christian man facing shyness.

"Just as shyness will compound itself, so, too, will one's confidence," explains Dr. Wenck. "Shy men, in small but steady doses, can build their confidence if they are willing to work at it. They can begin by approaching friendly people—a librarian, a minister, a bank teller— and asking for advice or help on some matter. Each week they can get to know more and more such people."

He adds, "They also should become members of small groups or clubs where they can be with a few people and not be overwhelmed by a large crowd." Church men's groups or service organizations can help men who are reserved become more self-assured.

Dr. Wenck admits that strange new surroundings and major life changes, like getting married, going into the military, or going to college, can cause the sort of anxiety that might lead to shyness in men. But that doesn't have to be the case.

"New situations offer as much opportunity for positive things to occur as they do negative things," says Dr. Wenck. "Maybe someone has been hesitant in other situations. Who cares? This is *now*. Strangers have no preconceived notions about men they meet. If the shy man will behave with confidence, he will be accepted as a capable and strong individual. It's a chance to start a new, more assertive life."

Pastors, psychologists, and other counselors generally agree that there is nothing baffling or mystical about overcoming shyness. Basically, there are five procedures that counselors suggest to men seeking help:

1. *Be yourself.* You have many unique and wonderful God-given personality traits that will attract people to you if you will just relax and behave naturally (Heb. 13:5).
2. *Don't exaggerate circumstances.* Don't develop needless anxiety about what "may" happen or what folks "might" think about you. These are manufactured worries. Keep your negative thoughts under control (Matt. 6:25).
3. *Be friendly.* You can find many new friends by first being friendly yourself. A simple handshake, a kind word, and a warm smile will go a long way in increasing social contacts for yourself (2 Chron. 10:7).
4. *Get a new view of yourself.* Learn to view your shortcomings as unique aspects of your character. No one except Jesus is perfect; nevertheless, everyone *is* unique. Capitalize on that (2 Tim. 1:7).
5. *Build confidence daily.* Try to accomplish something each day that will expand your circle of friends or expose you to new circumstances. Bite off a little at a time. Progress, no matter how little or how small, is better than standing still or regressing (James 1:2–3).

God has built into each of us some character elements that enable us to be properly cautious and logically careful. But He has not created us to be shy wallflowers who sit idly, eyes lowered, in back pews while others work and witness. Instead, we need to overcome bashfulness in order to become strong witnesses for Christ. Confronting bashfulness is not something from which we should shy away.

THINKING MORE ABOUT CHAPTER 18

Scripture Verses to Ponder

A man's wisdom maketh his face to shine, and the boldness of his face shall be changed.

—Ecclesiastes 8:1

Fear thou not; for I am with thee: be not dismayed; for I am thy God: I will strengthen thee; yea, I will help thee; yea, I will uphold thee with the right hand of my righteousness.

—Isaiah 41:10

For the Lord GOD will help me; therefore shall I not be confounded: therefore have I set my face like a flint, and I know that I shall not be ashamed.

—Isaiah 50:7

In [Christ] we have boldness and access with confidence by the faith of him.

—Ephesians 3:12

There is no fear in love; but perfect love casteth out fear: because fear hath torment. He that feareth is not made perfect in love.

—1 John 4:18

Questions to Consider

1. What are some things you can do to help in your church's visitation program if you seem too nervous to go on visits by yourself?
2. Jonah ran away in fear from the city of Ninevah. Peter denied three times that he knew Jesus. What other men from the Old and New Testaments can you think of who let fear overcome them? How did God restore these men to His service?
3. What are some things you can do to help visitors at your church or prayer group feel less intimidated about being in a strange environment?
4. Have you ever been asked to do something totally new, such as teach a Bible class or speak at a church function? What did you do to help control your nervousness and get past stage fright?
5. Moses lost the gift of oratory by not being obedient to God's directives. Have you ever gained or lost a spiritual gift by heeding or not heeding God's leading in your life? If so, what were those circumstances? How would you handle that same situation if it were to come up today? Do you know of any other man who may have had such a situation in his spiritual life?

SUGGESTED ADDITIONAL READINGS

Foster, Richard J. *Celebration of Discipline.* New York: Harper and Row, 1978.

Geisler, Norman L., and Paul K. Hoffman. *Why I Am a Christian.* Grand Rapids: Baker, 2000.

Green, Holly Wagner. *Turning Fear to Hope.* Grand Rapids: Zondervan, 1990.

Hensley, Dennis E. *Uncommon Sense: Fueling Success Skills with Enthusiasm.* Indianapolis: R & R Newkirk, 1984.

Kahn, Elayne, and David A. Rudnitsky. *1001 Ways to Reveal Your Personality.* New York: Signet, 1982.

CHAPTER 19

GET UP AND GROW

Mark Twain once wrote, "When I was 18, my father was the biggest fool I'd ever known. When I was 21, I was amazed at how much the old fellow had learned in just three years."

That's how life often is. We see changes occurring all around us but seldom realize that the most significant changes are taking place within us.

That's true of our growth as Christian men, too. Looking back over nearly five decades of living, only now do I realize that the seemingly overwhelming challenges and trials of previous years were really opportunities and experiences God was providing me for later use.

I'm now slower to react positively or negatively to life's circumstances. I wait for God's leading. I've grown and matured as a Christian; or, as I've confessed to my friends, I've come to realize that I've learned a lot since I've known it all.

My growth as a Christian can best be summarized in four words: *priorities, confidence, perspective,* and *forgiveness.*

PRIORITIES

The *priorities* of our Christian walk should begin with service to God. I learned to make God the first priority in my life after He proved to me that I was the first priority in His life.

In 1978, my wife had complications during labor while delivering our second child. Finally, the doctor told us our child would be still-born. We were emotionally crushed. We hugged each other and cried for hours. We were terribly distraught over the death of our baby.

Nine hours later my wife was taken into the delivery room to have the dead child removed. Miraculously, a faint heartbeat was discovered in our daughter. She was rushed to a special intensive care unit at Riley Children's Hospital in Indianapolis where, for days, she was treated around the clock.

And she lived. Today, she is a healthy and happy young woman who is active in music, drama, and various social and academic events at the elementary school where she is a music teacher for grades kindergarten through sixth. Each time my wife and I recall how close we came to losing Jeanette, our hearts are filled with incredible joy over the realization that she's here with us. How we love her!

With that in mind, I often sit in awe when I equate that event to the sacrifice God the Father made of His Son, Jesus. How *could* He yield His dearest Love for the likes of a sinner like me?

The only answer is that my salvation was the most important of all His priorities. Can I, then, make Him any less than my top priority? No, I dare not.

CONFIDENCE

My *confidence* as a Christian man has increased in measured amounts over the years. As a teenager, I was embarrassed even to stand in front of a group to share my testimony. Today, I teach Sunday school to a large class each week and lecture to hundreds of college students each year who attend Taylor University, where I am an English professor.

How did I gain this confidence? I spent nine years completing a Ph.D. in literature and linguistics. When the day came to defend my doctoral dissertation before a panel of five professors, I was eager and ready. I had prepared myself diligently, and, as a result, I sailed through the defense without a hitch.

It occurred to me then, as never before, that confidence as a Christian also came from preparation. The more grounded in the Word I became, the more able I would be to teach it, share it, and proclaim it. This led me to focus more time on prayer and Bible study. Shortly thereafter I was offered opportunities to teach fellow Christians. Preparation led to confidence, and confidence led to opportunity.

PERSPECTIVE

My *perspective* on my life as a Christian was gained during a twelve-month stint in South Vietnam as a sergeant in the U.S. Army. I worked as a chaplain's aide and bodyguard. The work was hard, the weather terrible, and the assignments often life-threatening. Through it all, however, I realized that my security in Christ was giving me comfort that many other soldiers did not have. I didn't relish the idea of being in a war zone, but I knew that God was with me and that He would use the experience to make me a better person.

In later years I faced certain hardships and setbacks—a lost job, an automobile accident, a facial paralysis, a bankrupt stock investment— but I was able to shrug each one off. "I lived through a war," I'd remind myself, "so what's this compared to that?" With that kind of perspective, I found I could handle anything life threw at me.

FORGIVENESS

And, finally, the development of *forgiveness* in my life helped me understand my continuous relationship with God. Prior to becoming a parent, I sometimes felt that the Bible was too nonchalant about forgiving sins. It taught that by confessing, repenting, and praying, we could receive forgiveness from God.

As a businessman, that baffled me.

Shouldn't there be more to the deal? I wondered. Shouldn't I have to offer some sort of trade-off or barter agreement?

After all, I came before God every day asking forgiveness of my sins. Surely His patience would eventually run short and He would want something more tangible, right?

Actually, no. Just asking for forgiveness was enough.

While rearing a family, when my son or daughter made a mistake or disobeyed me or fell short of my expectations, I never failed to say, "That's all right. I can see that you are really sorry."

My love for my children has always been boundless in its patience and forgiveness. How much more so must God's patience and forgiveness with and for me be.

With growth, I learn more each day about God. I'm spiritually more mature today than when I was twenty-four, but not nearly as mature in the Lord as I'll be when I'm sixty-four. I never intend to stop growing in His grace.

THINKING MORE ABOUT CHAPTER 19

Scripture Verses to Ponder

> But there is *forgiveness* with thee [God], that thou mayest be feared.
>   —Psalm 130:4 (emphasis added)

> For the LORD shall be thy *confidence.*
>   —Proverbs 3:26 (emphasis added)

> For thus saith the Lord GOD, . . . in quietness and in *confidence* shall be your strength. . . .
>   —Isaiah 30:15 (emphasis added)

Him [Jesus] hath God exalted with his right hand to be a Prince and a Saviour, for to give repentance to Israel, and *forgiveness* of sins.

—Acts 5:31 (emphasis added)

In whom we have redemption through his blood, even the *forgiveness* of sins.

—Colossians 1:14 (emphasis added)

Beloved, if our heart condemn us not, then have we *confidence* toward God.

—1 John 3:21 (emphasis added)

Questions to Consider

1. Do you ever have the feeling that everyone else—your boss, your business partner, your wife, your father or mother, your teacher, your client—is deciding what your priorities should be? Is this as it should be? What things do you think you can do to try to regain control of your own life priorities?

2. Have you ever failed miserably at something you attempted to accomplish? How did it make you feel? Was your confidence so shaken, you were afraid to try anything else? If so, what did you do to try to regain your self-confidence? What passages of Scripture helped you?

3. Have you ever become so caught up in something that it has caused you to lose perspective of other things around you? What effect does this have on your family members, Christian friends, and the people with whom you work? What steps can you take to insure that your life will have a good balance and that your view of things will be kept in proper perspective?

4. Have you ever had to go to someone and seek that person's forgiveness for something you had said or done? Why was this so difficult? What lessons did you learn from that experience?

How were you received by the person from whom you sought forgiveness?

5. Have you ever felt that someone who has sought your forgiveness was not worthy of a second chance? In what ways did Jesus give second chances to Peter, Matthew, Zacchaeus, the ten lepers, Lazarus, and others? What lessons about forgiveness can be learned from this?

SUGGESTED ADDITIONAL READINGS

Douglass, Stephan B., and Lee Roddy. *Making the Most of Your Mind.* San Bernardino: Here's Life, 1983.

Geisler, Norman, and Peter Bocchino. *Unshakable Foundations.* Minneapolis: Bethany House, 2000.

Hensley, Dennis E. *The Jesus Effect.* Boise: Pacific Press, 1991.

Hunt, Jane. *Seeing Yourself Through God's Eyes.* Grand Rapids: Zondervan/Pyranee, 1990.

Poland, Larry. *Rise to Conquer.* Chappaqua, New York: Christian Herald Books, 1979.

CHAPTER 20

AN INSTANT OF
UNDERSTANDING

Any of us who spend a fair amount of time on this earth can look back on our lives and recall a scattering of incidents wherein the realities of life came into immediate, sharp focus. Each of these "jolts of comprehension" was a mere flash—an instant of understanding—yet, it altered our perspectives on life in monumental ways.

When I was a boy, for example, I used to play "army" with my buddies. The rules were simple: if you got "shot," you had to fall down and count to sixty before you could get up and start playing again. If either side had all of its men down and counting at the same time, the other side won.

Many years later I was in the *real* army, carrying a *real* rifle, walking through a *real* jungle (Vietnam). In one sense, I understood that I was a soldier and that this was a real war. After all, I'd been given a uniform, I'd gone through basic training, and I was on foreign soil. I was prepared, right?

Well . . . not really. At 6:30 A.M. on February 8, 1971, I was on patrol six miles north of Long Binh. Our squad leader gave a hand signal indicating he had spotted something ahead of us. Instinctively, I crouched amidst some heavy foliage. Two seconds later the tree branches above me and the large fronds just over my head were shredded into a thousand pieces of leaf pulp as enemy machine-gun bullets riddled our position.

I'll never forget my reaction. I dropped forward on my knees, went white with terror, and sat motionless in wide-eyed shock. As though it was some great revelation, the thought went through my mind, *I could have been killed just then. Hey! This isn't "count to sixty and get up again." This is real war. Whoa! This is serious, man!*

Until that very instant, the understanding of what war was really like had been beyond my comprehension. Previously, I had read about war, heard others talk about it, had seen movies about it, and had even played it as a child. But not until those machine-gun bullets split the vegetation over my head did I *comprehend* war. From that instant on, I was a very changed soldier.

Throughout the Bible we have numerous examples of how God used various miracles to provide "an instant of understanding" to people about His sovereignty and power.

When Moses confronted Pharaoh and demanded the release of the Jews, he used power from God to turn a rod into a serpent, to bring frogs upon the land, and to turn water into blood. Using satanic power, the magicians of Pharaoh's court performed similar miracles.

However, when Moses smote the dust of the earth and transformed it into lice (and when he performed numerous other miraculous deeds), the court magicians found themselves absolutely powerless to match Jehovah's greatness. The Bible notes, "The magicians did . . . their enchantments to bring forth lice, but they could not" (Exod. 8:18).

As the magicians beat the dust and chanted their cultic rituals, they quickly noted that a greater power than Satan had chosen to nullify their abilities. In that instant, they were able to comprehend that the God of Moses was greater than the idols of the Egyptians. The Bible says they confessed Jehovah's greatness: "Then the magicians said unto Pharaoh, This is the finger of God" (Exod. 8:19).

That same hand of God provided other "instants" of understanding to other people regarding God's power. The inhabitants of Jericho had an instant of understanding when God sent fissures through their great wall and crumbled it. The citizens were so stunned, they didn't even fight back when the Israelites attacked (Josh. 6:21).

The Philistines had an instant of understanding when Goliath fell headlong to the ground, killed by a Jewish shepherd boy (1 Sam. 17:49). The prophets of Baal had their instant of understanding when God answered Elijah's prayer and sent fire from heaven to consume the bullock, altar, and water (1 Kings 18:38). The residents of Sodom and Gomorrah had their instant of understanding when they saw brimstone and fire drop on them from heaven (Gen. 19:24).

Other, more enlightening, instants of understanding are found in the New Testament. After traveling with Jesus and watching Him feed the multitudes, heal the sick, and cast out demons, the disciples were still not certain about His identity. So, one night Jesus asked them directly, "Who do men say that I, the Son of Man, am?"

To this, the disciples came up with a vast range of names—Old Testament prophets like Jeremiah and Elijah, current wandering preachers like John the Baptist—all sorts of responses. But then Jesus asked them who the disciples, themselves, thought He was. No one spoke, except for Peter. In that instant everything became totally clear to him, and (as usual) he spoke his mind: "Thou art the Christ, the Son of the living God" (Matt. 16:16).

Peter's life was changed forever at that moment. Even when the flesh would later fail him, his spirit would rebound time and again to do new service for the Lord.

As dramatic as all of these examples are, a far greater instant of understanding lies just one breath away for each of us. Sooner or later, everyone must die (Heb. 9:27). In the moment after death there will be an instant understanding of who God is. For the believer, it will be an immediate time of blessed fellowship with Christ in heaven (2 Cor. 5:8). Right now, in our earthly bodies, we can only imagine how wonderful this experience will be, but we will never be able to comprehend it until that "instant" actually occurs.

For the person lost in sin, however, it will also be an instant of understanding, but one permeated with horror and agony. Christ warned the hypocrites and sinners, "How can ye escape the damnation of hell?" (Matt. 23:33).

We can either go to Him now, or wait until He calls us . . . an "instant" from now.

THINKING MORE ABOUT CHAPTER 20

Scripture Verses to Ponder

> And the magicians did so with their enchantments to bring forth lice, but they could not: so there were lice upon man, and upon beast. Then the magicians said unto Pharaoh, This is the finger of God: and Pharaoh's heart was hardened, and he hearkened not unto them; as the LORD had said.
> —Exodus 8:18–19

> So the people shouted when the priests blew with the trumpets: and it came to pass, when the people heard the sound of the trumpet, and the people shouted with a great shout, that the wall fell down flat, so that the people went up into the city, every man straight before him, and they took the city.
> —Joshua 6:20

> Therefore David ran, and stood upon the Philistine, and took his sword, and drew it out of the sheath thereof, and slew him, and cut off his head therewith. And when the Philistines saw their champion was dead, they fled.
> —1 Samuel 17:51

Questions to Consider

1. What instants of understanding have you had in your life? Were you ever in a serious automobile accident? in the midst of a burning building? trapped in an elevator? dismissed from a good job? Take a moment to recall these events in your life. How did God use these shocking or revealing circumstances to help you see life in a different light?

2. During a time of crisis, people react in various ways: some may cry and wail, some may panic and run, some may stay calm and begin to take steps to handle the crisis. Why do you feel people react in such diverse ways? How can having the peace of Christ within you help you to face any situation with confidence and calmness?

3. Do you think it is possible to experience an instant of understanding, yet ignore the lesson it presents? Why, for instance, did Pharaoh's magicians recognize God's power yet continue to serve Pharaoh? Why, for that matter, did Pharaoh's heart remain hardened?

4. Can an instant of understanding be passed on to someone else? Having read this chapter, have the lessons had an impact on you? If you tell your children or friends about an instant of understanding that you experienced, will it have an effect on them?

5. When Peter proclaimed Jesus to be the Messiah, Jesus said it was because God the Father had revealed this to Peter. Do you think most instants of understanding come from God or just from basic human experiences?

SUGGESTED ADDITIONAL READINGS

Bavinck, Herman. *Our Reasonable Faith.* Grand Rapids: Eerdmans, 1956.

Hemfelt, Robert, and Paul Warren. *Kids Who Carry Our Pain.* Nashville: Nelson, 1990.

Hutchcraf, Ron. *Called to Greatness.* Chicago: Moody, 2000.

Packer, J. I. *Evangelism and the Sovereignty of God.* Downers Grove, Ill.: InterVarsity, 1961.

Rubenstein, C. M., and P. Shaver. *In Search of Intimacy.* New York: Delacorte Press, 1982.

Wheat, Ed. *Love Life for Every Married Couple.* Grand Rapids: Zondervan, 1978.

CHAPTER 21

YOU ARE WHAT YOU EAT

Dietitians tell us that men become walking examples of what they eat. By that, they mean that men who consume large amounts of fatty meats, candy, cakes, starchy breads, and potatoes will look overweight, whereas men who drink skim milk and eat whole grains and fresh fruits and vegetables will look trim and fit.

I believe a parallel to this can be drawn regarding our spiritual diets. What we consume in order to nurture our spirits will reflect whether those spirits are receiving a balanced diet or are suffering from spiritual malnutrition. To illustrate this, let me tell you a "diet story" from the Old Testament.

Not long after being made king of Israel, Saul and six hundred of his soldiers went to war against the Philistines. While out scouting, Saul's son Jonathan noticed a point of vulnerability in the Philistine defenses at Michmash. He and his armor bearer made an impromptu foray against the enemy. They caught the Philistines off-guard and were able to slay twenty of them. This caused a panic in the Philistine camp, making the soldiers flee in retreat.

Sensing an opportunity for a victory when he saw the Philistines suddenly running away, Saul ordered his men to attack. To insure that his soldiers would make the most of the battle, Saul ordered that the men were to fight all day and not even stop to eat. If any man ate, he would be executed.

Many hours later, after much fighting and a great victory, the Jewish soldiers came walking back to camp. They were exhausted and hungry, but no man would eat, fearing the king's order. Jonathan, however, had not been around when the order had been issued, so he hadn't heard it. As such, when he passed through a wooded area where honeycombs were hanging in trees, he extended his staff to one and pulled down a thick glob of honey.

Jonathan hungrily swallowed the honey. Almost instantly his body responded to the influx of natural sugar and vitamins. He felt new energy flow through his body. Even his weary eyes popped wide open and were revived (1 Sam. 14:27).

The other soldiers immediately told Jonathan about Saul's order. Jonathan saw no logic to it, so he countermanded it and told his men to feed themselves on the captured animals of the enemy. He told them that the battle was over, that they had fought hard and had won, and that it was only fair they should be fed properly.

When word of this reached Saul, he felt that his authority had been challenged. He ordered Jonathan to be executed. Instead of carrying out this order, the soldiers reminded Saul that had it not been for Jonathan's cunning and bravery, there would never have been a victory that day. They refused to kill the hero of the day; Saul was forced to drop the matter.

The Bible does not exaggerate the situation when it says that the honey completely revived Jonathan's physical body. Honey consists of 76 percent naturally refined sugar (energy). Honey also contains vitamin C, seven of the B vitamins, and a variety of important minerals. And, since honey is already refined, its nutritional components enter the body's system very rapidly. It's an instant "picker upper."

SPIRITUAL HONEY

Perhaps there have been days when you have felt as spiritually exhausted as Jonathan felt physically exhausted. Maybe you've wished you could ingest something that would instantly rejuvenate your soul the same way the honey rejuvenated Jonathan's body.

Well, the Bible claims that there is such a thing, and it is the Word of God. "How sweet are thy words unto my taste! yea, *sweeter* than honey to my mouth" (Ps. 119:103, emphasis added). Reading and meditating on God's Word is even more refreshing to the soul than honey is to the body. This is so because "man doth not live by bread only, but by every word that proceedeth out of the mouth of the LORD" (Deut. 8:3).

If we miss our regular church services, Bible study group meetings, or daily devotional times, we will be robbing our soul of its needed nourishment. Without nourishment, our soul will grow weary; it will become frail and weak. It needs to be given spiritual food—water, bread, honey—from the Word of God.

Jesus was the Word of God made flesh (John 1:1–2). By turning to the Word (Christ), our spiritual diet is always balanced. Jeremiah said that God was "the fountain of living waters" (Jer. 2:13), and Jesus confirmed that this referred to Him: "If any man thirst, let him come unto me, and drink . . . rivers of living water" (John 7:37–38). Jesus also explained that He was the bread of life (Luke 22:19).

If it is true, in a physical sense, that we are what we eat, it is equally true in a spiritual sense. If you feel spiritually depressed, give yourself a quick physical. Are you reading your Bible? Are you memorizing verses (Ps. 119:11)? Are you fellowshipping in the Word with other believers? Are you sharing the Word with lost souls?

If you answer no to these questions, give yourself a good dose of spiritual honey. You'll feel the effect immediately.

O taste and see that the LORD is good.

—Psalm 34:8

THINKING MORE ABOUT CHAPTER 21

Scripture Verses to Ponder

Thy word have I hid in mine heart, that I might not sin against thee.

—Psalm 119:11

For my people have committed two evils; they have forsaken me the fountain of living *waters*, and hewed them out cisterns, broken cisterns, that can hold no water.

—Jeremiah 2:13

And he took *bread*, and gave thanks, and brake it, and gave unto them, saying, This is my body which is given for you: this do in remembrance of me.

—Luke 22:19 (emphasis added)

In the beginning was the Word, and the Word was with God, and the Word was God. The same was in the beginning with God.

—John 1:1–2

Questions to Consider

1. It has been said, "You are what you eat." What about other things we take in? Does what we hear and see have an impact on what we turn out to be? Take a moment and make some notes about how messages you "ingest" can change you.
   • Television shows:
   • Music:
   • Books and magazines:
   • Conversations:
   • Billboards and newspaper ads:
   • Campaign pins and bumper stickers:

2. Whenever we overeat, we feel uncomfortable and sometimes even get sick. Have you ever overeaten of the world's pleasures and found yourself heartsick, ashamed, and uncomfortable later?
3. This chapter showed us how there are two ways to nourish the body: with food and with God's Word. If you want an opportunity to share the Word of God with someone, what about inviting that person to your home for a meal? Meet both needs.

SUGGESTED ADDITIONAL READINGS

Black, David Alan, and David S. Dockery. *Interpreting the New Testament*. Nashville: Broadman-Holman, 2000.

Brandt, Henry. *The Struggle for Peace.* Wheaton, Ill.: Scripture Press, 1965.

Christensen, Evelyn. *"Lord, Change Me!"* Wheaton, Ill.: Victor Books, 1977.

Faber, Carl A. *On Listening.* Pacific Palisades, Calif.: Perseus Books, 1976.

Hemphill, Ken. *The Names of God.* Nashville: Broadman-Holman, 2000.

LaHaye, Tim. *How to Study the Bible for Yourself.* Eugene, Ore.: Harvest House, 1976.

McDowell, Josh. *Guide to Understanding Your Bible.* San Bernardino, Calif.: Here's Life, 1982.

CHAPTER 22

TRACING YOUR SPIRITUAL GENEALOGY

Ever since the success of Alex Haley's *Roots* in the 1970s, people have seemed eager to delve into their family genealogies. A friend of mine, Rev. Tim Franklin, showed me a different kind of genealogical tracing. Tim made a trace of his *spiritual* genealogy to discover how many people were in a chain of Christians who led to himself. Here's how it worked.

When Tim was a boy, his older brother Gordon explained the plan of salvation to him. Later, at a Christian summer camp, Tim yielded his life to the Lord. Thanks to his brother's witnessing and concern, Tim was saved.

Gordon, himself, had been saved at a revival meeting where Billy Graham had explained how young people could live their lives for Jesus.

Billy Graham had been led to the Lord after listening to a sermon by Mordicai Ham, who, himself, had been saved while attending a revival crusade conducted by Billy Sunday.

Billy Sunday had been saved through the ministry of Wilbur Chapman, who, previously, had been led to Christ by a preacher named F. B. Meyer.

F. B. Meyer had been turned from a life as a National Free Church social reformer in England to a crusader for Jesus after attending a message preached in a Wesleyan chapel by visiting American evangelist Dwight L. Moody.

The man who started this great 140-year chain of revivalist preachers was a man very few people have ever heard of. His name was Edward Kimball. He was a tall bachelor who, at age thirty, worked as a shoe salesman in Boston. Kimball was a rather quiet, unobtrusive man. He was a walking testimony for Christ in all that he did, though not in a confrontational or self-righteous way.

Kimball was an orthodox Congregationalist who taught a Sunday school class for teenage boys at Mount Vernon Church in Boston. At the time, D. L. Moody, age seventeen, was living with relatives in Boston while he worked as a clerk at Holton's Shoe Store. His relatives demanded that Moody attend Mount Vernon Church with them. Moody consented, not out of any love of religion but merely to maintain his room and board.

In late May of 1854, Moody made his first appearance at Mount Vernon Church and was put in Edward Kimball's class. Kimball welcomed Moody graciously. Moody appreciated Kimball's kindness, but he felt like a fish out of water. The other boys all knew each other, had grown up together, and were obviously comfortable in a church setting. As for Moody, he simply wanted to go through the motions and get out as soon as possible.

Kimball handed Moody a Bible, then instructed the class to turn to the gospel of John. Everyone quickly found the reference, except Moody. He was flipping one page at a time, starting in Genesis.

The other boys chuckled at Moody's lack of knowledge, but one admonishing glare from Mr. Kimball quickly silenced their rudeness. Kimball gave his own Bible to Moody, already opened to John, and he took Moody's Bible for his own use. Moody was so grateful for the rescue, he later said, "I vowed right then to stick by this fellow who had stuck by me."

For the next eleven months Moody continued to attend Kimball's class, but he said very little and certainly made no profession of faith.

Away from church, Moody had a foul mouth. He spent no time reading the Bible. His only goal was to remain what he had become: namely,
the top shoe salesman in Boston. Still, Kimball knew that Moody's
mind was fertile and that for eleven months seeds of biblical wisdom
had been sown there.

During a week of revival meetings in April of 1855, Edward Kimball's
spirit became greatly burdened for Dwight L. Moody. On Saturday
morning, April 21, Kimball left his rooming house and walked downtown to ask Moody, now eighteen, to accept Christ as his Savior. This
was not easy for Kimball, for he was a reserved, nonconfrontational
person. Still, his heart was burdened for Moody's salvation.

Kimball entered Holton's and went directly to the back of the store.
There he found Moody stacking shoe boxes.

"I went up to him and put my hand on his shoulder," Kimball later
recalled. "I asked him to come to Christ, who loved him and who
wanted his love, and *should* have it in a developing relationship."

Kimball was so genuine in his imploring, tears came into his eyes.
Moody recognized the sincere concern of this man and was convinced
of the verity of Kimball's own faith.

"It seemed that Moody was just ready for the light that broke upon
him," said Kimball, "for there, at once, in the back of that shoe store in
Boston, he gave himself and his life to Christ."

Kimball continued to be Moody's biblical mentor, and in March of
1856, Moody joined Mount Vernon Church. He had changed his talk
and his walk. He spent every spare moment reading the Bible.

In September of that year Moody transferred to Chicago to work
for a Midwest branch of Holton's Shoe Store. It was here that he would
accept a great call from God to initiate a campaign of global evangelism.

Moody and Kimball were not destined to see each other again.

Still, it didn't matter, for the great wave of revival momentum that
Kimball had caused to swell was well under way by then. Kimball had
led Moody to Christ, and Moody was now leading literally tens of
thousands of others to Christ . . . one of whom would be F. B. Meyer
. . . who, in turn, was destined to lead Wilbur Chapman to Christ . . .
who, in his time, would continue this wonderful spiritual genealogy

until it would ultimately reach Gordon Franklin and then his brother Tim Franklin, as well.

Did Kimball have any notion that his witnessing to D. L. Moody would lead to the creation of a succession of world-renowned evangelists? No, of course not. His only burden was to free one teenage boy from the shackles of sin. Nevertheless, by doing so, the Lord magnified the blessing a millionfold.

Not everyone is called to be a platform evangelist. Some, like Kimball, are called to lead one person at a time to God. As the apostle Paul explained, "I planted, Apollos watered, but God was causing the growth" (1 Cor. 3:6 NASB). Similarly, Kimball could have said, "I planted, Moody and those who came after him watered, and God caused the growth."

This should serve as a constant source of motivation for all of us who serve the Lord, no matter how humble our calling may appear to be. It may be that the Lord will use us to touch *one* life that will, in turn, touch another, that will, in turn, touch yet another life, and so on for several generations.

Wouldn't it be grand if, at some future date, some saved person sat down and traced his or her spiritual genealogy and found that it had begun with *you*?

THINKING MORE ABOUT CHAPTER 22

Scripture Verses to Ponder

Thou gavest also thy good spirit to instruct them.

—Nehemiah 9:20

Come, ye children, hearken unto me: I will teach you the fear of the LORD.

—Psalm 34:11

Now there are diversities of gifts, but the same Spirit.
                                                —1 Corinthians 12:4

Yet in the church I had rather speak five words with my understanding, that by my voice I might teach others also, than ten thousand words in an unknown tongue.
                                                —1 Corinthians 14:19

For he that soweth to his flesh shall of the flesh reap corruption; but he that soweth to the Spirit shall of the Spirit reap life everlasting.
                                                —Galatians 6:8

Look not every man on his own things, but every man also on the things of others.
                                                —Philippians 2:4

Questions to Consider

1. Have you ever tried to trace your own spiritual genealogy? How far back can you go? Where and when were you led to Christ, and who was the person most responsible for helping you learn to trust the Lord? Maybe you could contact this person and ask him or her to share with you how he or she was led to Christ.
2. Have you ever spent time reading biographies of great heroes of the faith? Perhaps by discovering how these people were led to Jesus, you will discover some of the steps by which you, too, found your way into the kingdom.
3. Can you see a way in which studying your biological family history might provide insights into your spiritual life? For example, in tracing the *human* genealogy of Jesus (Matt. 1:1–25), we can see that his ancestors included a murderer and his adulteress wife (David and Bathsheba), among other less savory individuals. This shows that God allows us to rise above anything in our

family's past that other people might hold against us. We are unique individuals in God's sight.

4. Looking forward in time, what are some of the legacies of spirituality you would like to pass on to the next generation of Christians? (E.g., a passion for God's Word, a ministry to lost souls, a walking testimony at work, etc.) Make your own list.

SUGGESTED ADDITIONAL READINGS

Boice, James Montgomery. *Ordinary Men Called by God.* Wheaton, Ill.: Victor Books, 1988.

Hyman, B. D. *My Mother's Keeper.* New York: William Morrow and Co., 1985.

Who Was Who in America. Chicago: Marquis, 1993.

Who's Who Among Bible Women. Springfield, Mo.: Gospel Publishing House, 1979.

Who's Who in Genealogy. Detroit: Gale Research, 1992.

Who's Who in the Bible. New York: Philosophical Library, 1986.

Who's Who in the Talmud. Middle Village, N.Y.: Jonathan David, 1985.

CHAPTER 23

TOO OBVIOUS TO ACCEPT AS TRUTH

I was recently asked why I am willing to share my testimony and willing to explain the plan of salvation to people who had already rejected my appeal many times. My response was, "Because sometimes the truth is so simple, so obvious, and so basic, people just cannot comprehend or accept it the first time they hear it."

This was just as true in the apostle Paul's day as it is now. Paul went to great lengths to explain the plan of salvation to Herod Agrippa II, the Tetrarch of North Palestine. Paul shared his testimony, explained every detail of his miraculous conversion, and then offered to lead Agrippa to Christ. Agrippa was swayed at first, but in the end he resisted. "*Almost* thou persuadest me to be a Christian," he told Paul, but then backed off (Acts 26:28, emphasis added).

Actually, I can relate to Agrippa's skepticism. Most people believe in the adage, "If it sounds too good to be true, it probably is."

Not long after I was first married, my father-in-law told me about a donkey basketball game that was being planned as a fund-raising event at a local school. The whole thing sounded preposterous to me: two teams of men trying to compete against each other while riding over the basketball court on donkeys.

I felt sure my father-in-law was pulling my leg. No matter how many times he explained the event to me, I still responded, "I'm not falling for that. You're just trying to trick me into buying a ticket so that you can have a good laugh at my expense." So, my father-in-law paid for the tickets, took me to the game the next week, and—lo and behold!—men *really did* get up on donkeys and played basketball that way. I laughed myself silly. It was . . . well, almost unbelievable. Yet, it was true. I saw it.

SOMETHING'S FISHY HERE

A similar thing happened to me not long after that. My cousin Stanley, then fourteen, came from Tennessee to Michigan to be a groomsman in my brother's wedding. Stanley was an avid fisherman and had caught every game fish that swam in Tennessee waters. Stanley hadn't, however, spent any time in the North.

One evening as we were getting into my car to drive to the wedding rehearsal, Stanley saw three ice-fishing poles hanging on our garage wall. They were wooden sticks, two-and-a-half feet long, and painted bright blue.

"What are these things?" he asked, pointing.

"Ice-fishing poles," I answered. "You attach a line to the end, chop a hole in the ice, and then drop the line in."

Stanley looked at me, grinned, and said, "Seriously, man, what are these?"

"I *am* being serious," I insisted. "They're ice-fishing poles."

"Right," he said, dubiously. "If that's so, where's the reel?"

"You don't need one," I explained. "If you get a bite, you just pull up the line hand over hand. Or, you can hang onto the pole, jump up, run away from the ice hole, and as you run, the line will pull the fish up to the surface."

This caused Stanley to laugh uproariously. The very idea of a fisherman running away from his catch was a truly comedic scene to him.

When he finally caught his breath, he said, "And I suppose the reason the pole is wooden instead of fiberglass is so that you can give the line a good, quick jerk and snag the fish as soon as you feel a bite, eh?"

I nodded enthusiastically. "Right, right. That's it."

He shook his head. "Man, I've heard some whoppers in my time, but that ice-fishing story tops them all," he told me, still chuckling. Then he paused a moment and asked again, "So, really now, what are these things?"

I shrugged my shoulders. "I don't know what else to tell you," I said. "They're ice-fishing poles."

During the drive across town, I retold the procedures for ice fishing. Stanley still thought I was teasing him. He didn't believe me. In fact, the next day I had to get my brother and my dad to verify to Stanley that what I had said was true. And, even then, he had to be given a demonstration of how to attach the fishing line and how to use an ice spud to chop the holes in the ice.

To Stanley, trying to fish with a miniature wooden stick was as unbelievable as it had seemed, to me, to play basketball while riding a donkey. People had given us honest, direct, simple explanations of these things, yet they seemed "too obvious" to be true.

RESISTANCE TO NEW IDEAS

Even Jesus ran into this problem. When Christ explained to Nicodemus the concept of "new birth" salvation, the old priest thought Jesus was playing word games with him (John 3:1–12).

"How can a man be born when he is old?" asked Nicodemus (v. 4). He thought Jesus was suggesting something impossible. Nicodemus argued with Jesus, saying it was ludicrous to imagine a full-grown man trying to go back into his mother's womb in order to go through the birthing process again.

Slowly, patiently, Jesus had to help Nicodemus separate the process of physical birth from spiritual birth. It took time, but eventually Nicodemus was able to grasp the concept.

Should we be any less patient, less diligent, than Jesus was in explaining and re-explaining the salvation process to those who find it hard to accept? I believe we honor the Lord when we steadfastly represent Him to those who are skeptical, cautious, and resistant.

It has been my experience that the most effective way to reach resistant unbelievers is to follow a three-step procedure:

1. Offer an *explanation* of the plan of salvation in a very simple, easy-to-follow way. Use the "Romans Road" or the "Four Spiritual Laws" or the "wordless book" or any of numerous other ways that have been developed to make one-on-one evangelism easy. Pass along a tract or a New Testament. The main thing is to keep things uncomplicated during the initial contact.

2. Give a *demonstration* of the Christian life in all that you say and do. Most men who will resist your initial invitation to accept Christ will want time to consider how this might alter their lives. By observing you, they should be able to discern a life of contentment, joy, fulfillment, and purpose. Seeing often leads to believing.

3. Provide a frequent *reiteration* of your beliefs. Continue to share your testimony, to distribute tracts, to respond to questions put to you about Christ, and to witness to the lost. Try to keep in mind that what you are explaining is a totally new concept to most unbelievers, something that is alien to their way of thinking. It will take time for them to "reprogram" their perception of things. But, like the diligent salesperson who knocks on the same door many times and is finally rewarded for his persistence by getting a sale, we, too, will often be rewarded if we are consistent in stressing the merits of the Christian life.

THE HARDENED HEART

I wish I could say that this three-step process could guarantee success in soul-winning. I can't. It is very effective, but not fail-proof.

And that's because, despite all your sincerity and imploring, some people will have hardened their hearts to a degree of total resistance. How sad, but how true. The fault does not lie in your inability to witness but rather in their inability to be teachable.

Jesus faced such a person in Pontius Pilate. The Roman governor asked Jesus if He was the Messiah, this "king" the Jews had been prophesying would one day come. Jesus responded that what Pilate had said was true. To this, in a mocking jest, Pilate challenged Jesus with a counterpoint question: "What is truth?"

To open such a debate with Jesus at this point was an exercise in futility. Pilate's question merited no answer, and, for a fact, Jesus did not dignify it with a response.

Pilate had not been living in a cave. He was governor of Judea. He knew about *everything* that went on in his region. Certainly he had heard of the countless miracles Jesus had performed; he knew about the sermons, teachings, and fulfillment of prophesy Jesus had provided; he may even have been told that Jesus referred to Himself as "the way, the *truth,* and the life" (John 14:6, emphasis added). As such, to ask Jesus to explain "truth" was pointless. If all of these other acts of Jesus had not made "the truth" clear and obvious to Pilate, nothing ever would. His heart just wasn't teachable.

Our responsibility is to explain the plan of salvation to lost souls and then to pray for the Holy Spirit to soften the hearts of individuals so that they will become teachable. Even if our words are not heeded, Christ is still honored by our diligence. As such, as long as there is the slightest response, I feel we should continue to witness to resistant people.

I even keep an ice-fishing pole in my home office to remind me of that.

THINKING MORE ABOUT CHAPTER 23

Scripture Verses to Ponder

He shall cover thee with his feathers, and under his wings shalt thou trust: his *truth* shall be thy shield and buckler.
                                              —Psalm 91:4 (emphasis added)

The truth of the LORD endureth for ever. Praise ye the LORD.
                                              —Psalm 117:2

Nicodemus saith unto him, How can a man be born when he is old? can he enter the second time into his mother's womb, and be born? Jesus answered, Verily, verily, I say unto thee, Except a man be born of water and of the Spirit, he cannot enter into the kingdom of God. That which is born of flesh is flesh; and that which is born of the Spirit is spirit. Marvel not that I said unto thee, Ye must be born again. The wind bloweth where it listeth, and thou hearest the sound thereof, but canst not tell whence it cometh, and whither it goeth: so is every one that is born of the Spirit.
                                              —John 3:4–8

Jesus saith unto him, I am the way, the truth, and the life: no man cometh unto the Father, but by me.
                                              —John 14:6

Questions to Consider

1. Have your ever thought about how often man changes his opinion on what "truth" is? For many centuries, people were taught that the earth was flat, but this "truth" was proved false after the voyages of Columbus. More recently, people were told that light could not bend, but thanks to modern fiber optics, light now

can be bent. Man's truth is constantly in a state of revision, but the truth of God's Word is unchanging eternally.

2. Courtrooms can be very intense places. Have you ever been sworn in as a witness in a case? You are cautioned to tell the "whole truth and nothing but the truth." When you turn to God during your prayer time, are you obedient in confessing the "whole truth and nothing but the truth" about your life? He wants to share your burdens and relieve you of your sins, but for Him to do so, you must have an honest relationship with God.

3. Even as a believer, are there sections in the Bible that you find hard to comprehend, perhaps even hard to believe? Don't feel ashamed about that. Instead, make notes about those passages and discuss them with your pastor, Sunday school teacher, or a senior saint in the Lord. There is strength to be gained by understanding God's Word.

4. Are there any parts of your life in which you feel you have taken unfair advantage of someone by being less than truthful with that person? If so, today would be a good day to do something about making amends for your poor behavior.

SUGGESTED ADDITIONAL READINGS

Gettys, Joseph Miller. *How to Enjoy Studying the Bible.* Atlanta: John Knox Press, 1962.

Moody, Dwight L. *Prevailing Prayer.* Chicago: Moody, n.d.

Pink, Arthur Walkington. *Profiting from the Word.* London: Banner of Truth Trust, 1974.

Richards, Lawrence O. *Creative Bible Study.* Grand Rapids: Zondervan, 1971.

Stott, John R. W. *Your Mind Matters.* London: InterVarsity, 1972.

Toler, Stan, and Debra White Smith. *The Harder I Laugh, the Deeper I Hurt.* Kansas City: Beacon Hill Press, 2000.

CHAPTER 24

IF LIFE'S A JUNGLE,
BECOME A TRAILBLAZER

Throughout the city of Fort Wayne, Indiana, where I live, you can find statues, parks, shopping malls, schools, and playgrounds named in honor of John Chapman (1774–1845).

Chapman spent nearly half a century wandering the Midwest planting apple orchards. Settlers dubbed him "Johnny Appleseed," and he was welcomed at campsites wherever he went. He was loved because people knew that wherever Johnny Appleseed walked, he left his mark on the land in the form of blossoming apple trees and delicious fruit.

Have you ever stopped to wonder how the trail of *your* life has been marked? What evidences of your life's wanderings have you left behind you?

Experienced woodsmen say it's impossible for a person to walk through a forest and not leave some kind of trail signs. Walking through life is like that, too. No one can be totally inconspicuous.

I was recently watching a television special about nuclear submarines. The narrator explained that even though these submarines can run with virtually soundless engines and can dive miles below the ocean's surface, they still can be trailed at night. This is because as the submarine churns through the deep ocean water, it drives millions of phosphorescent plankton to the surface. Reconnaissance satellites can detect this two-mile trail of glowing sea life that is left in the wake of the submarine. Even in the ocean, man's trail is marked.

The whole theme of the classic movie *It's a Wonderful Life* is that— for better or for worse—each man leaves a mark on the trail he walks in life. A person may think he is inconsequential (as did the Jimmy Stewart character in the movie), but that simply isn't so. Each of us is having an influence on everything and everyone around us.

THE PATH OF RIGHTEOUSNESS

Knowing this to be true, it behooves us to study some of the lessons Jesus taught about walking along life's trail.

To begin with, Jesus was not an isolationist. His people, the Jews, despised the Samaritans and would not set foot in Samaria. But Jesus was a friend to all. He purposely walked both to *and through* Samaria (John 4:4). He shared the plan of salvation with many Samaritans and they "believed because of his own word" (v. 41).

By assisting with mission works, both at home and abroad, we, too, can show ourselves willing to walk among strangers and willing to share the plan of salvation with those who might otherwise be isolated from God's Word. In our wake, we can leave many redeemed souls.

Secondly, Jesus taught us to walk in light. This meant to walk according to His teachings and personal example. "I am the light of the world: he that followeth me shall not walk in darkness" (John 8:12). This is reminiscent of the psalmist's praise of the Scripture when he wrote, "Thy word is a lamp unto my feet, and a light unto my path" (Ps. 119:105).

Many times there are forks in the path of life. We may be confused over whether to turn left or right. The decision is made easier by casting the light of the Lord's teachings on the paths. If the light reveals the world's evil, we know we need to redirect our steps.

Thirdly, our walk for Christ should clear a path for others to follow to the Savior. John the Baptist prepared a path for men to travel to Christ (Luke 3:4). John wandered the wilderness, leaving behind him a trail of sermons, baptismal services, and proclamations of Christ's coming.

Similarly, the apostle Paul traveled throughout Asia Minor and southern Europe, leaving behind him many newly established churches in all of the cities he visited.

How is the trail of your life marked? Do you consider yourself a Kit Carson of Christianity? Have you blazed any new trails for the cause of Christ lately?

The apple orchards originally planted 150 years ago by Johnny Appleseed helped to feed the pioneers as they traveled westward. Those orchards, however, have long since died off.

In contrast, the seeds of Christianity planted nearly two thousand years ago in Greece and Italy by the apostle Paul are *still* flourishing and have since spread to Europe, England, and all the known world.

There is an important lesson to be learned here: we can mark our trails in many ways, but only our efforts to serve the Lord will have any lasting effect. Hack through a jungle with a machete and the vegetation will grow back within days; but cut a path through sin with the "sword of the Lord," and the trail will remain visible for ages on end.

THINKING MORE ABOUT CHAPTER 24

Scripture Verses to Ponder

I am the Almighty God; walk before me, and be thou perfect.
—Genesis 17:1

Thy word is a lamp unto my feet, and a light unto my path.
—Psalm 119:105

The word of God came unto John the son of Zacharias in the wilderness. And he came into all the country about Jordan, preaching the baptism of repentance for the remission of sins; As it is written in the book of the words of [Isaiah] the prophet, saying, The voice of one crying in the wilderness, Prepare ye the way of the Lord, make his paths straight.

—Luke 3:2–4

He left Judea, and departed again into Galilee. And he must needs go through Samaria. Then cometh he to a city of Samaria, which is called Sychar, near to the parcel of ground that Jacob gave to his son Joseph.

—John 4:3–5

I must work the works of him that sent me, while it is day: the night cometh, when no man can work. As long as I am in the world, I am the light of the world.

—John 9:4–5

Questions to Consider

1. Enoch walked a trail with God. Because of it, he was translated from earth to heaven and did not have to die. Have you heard how one little girl explained it? She said, "Enoch liked to walk and talk with God every day. One day he walked and walked and walked until he was so far away from home he knew he couldn't get back before dark. When he told this to God, the Lord said, 'Oh, well, just come on home with me then.'"

2. Are you blazing any trails for the Lord these days? Are you walking for God in your neighborhood, at work, at social gatherings, on business trips, while on vacation, when visiting friends and relatives? There is no reason why you shouldn't be; after all, God's right there next to you wherever you go.

3. In this chapter we talked about the trail blazed by the apostle

Paul. Can you think of other Christians who have walked a perilous path for the cause of Christ and have accomplished great
things in doing so?

4. In American history we pay tribute to people such as Lewis and
Clark, Daniel Boone, Kit Carson, and other explorers and scouts.
These people had to be courageous, curious, determined, and
optimistic. What sort of characteristics should a man have if he
wishes to explore new places for the cause of Christ?

SUGGESTED ADDITIONAL READINGS

Cook, William H. *Success, Motivation and the Scriptures.* Nashville:
Broadman, 1974.

Douglass, Stephen B. *Managing Yourself.* San Bernardino, Calif.: Here's
Life, 1978.

Ellis, Barbara. *How to Get Ahead and Still Like Yourself.* Indianapolis:
R & R Newkirk, 1982.

Hunt, Gladys. *It's Alive.* Wheaton, Ill.: Harold Shaw, 1971.

Morley, Patrick. *Coming Back to God.* Grand Rapids: Zondervan, 2000.

Patterson, Ben. *Deepening Your Conversation with God.* Minneapolis:
Bethany House, 2000.

Poland, Larry. *Rise to Conquer.* Chappaqua, N.Y.: Christian Herald
Books, 1979.

CHAPTER 25

THE APOSTLE JOHN'S "TEN MUST WANTED" LIST

Long before the FBI developed its "Ten Most Wanted" list, the apostle John prepared a "Ten *Must* Wanted" list. There are ten specific references in the book of John that explain what a devoted Christian must want as his priorities in life. Reminding ourselves on a regular basis of what these "musts" are can provide spiritual motivation for us.

1. John 3:7, "You *must* be born again" (NIV, emphasis added). Jesus explained to Nicodemus that people need to have a spiritual rebirth in themselves. Upon accepting Christ as Savior, individuals are washed spiritually clean by the cleansing blood of Jesus. The old sin nature is banished and is replaced by the indwelling of the Holy Spirit. Christians become new creations.
2. John 3:14, ". . . the Son of Man *must* be lifted up" (NIV, emphasis added). It was necessary for Christ to be willingly nailed to the cross and to be lifted high before mankind as the sacrificial lamb. Those who look upon Him and believe in His atoning power will be saved.

3. John 3:30, "He *must* increase, but I *must* decrease" (emphasis added). John the Baptist preached diligently and vehemently to his followers that the coming of Christ was at hand. When that blessed event transpired, John willingly faded into the background in order to allow the attention to be turned to Christ.

4. John 3:30, "He *must* increase, but I *must* decrease" (emphasis added). Similarly, although we may serve in highly visible ministries as pastors, deacons, elders, Sunday school teachers, or youth workers, in all actions everything should be focused on Jesus. He is the Master, and we are the servants.

5. John 4:4, "He *must* needs go through Samaria" (emphasis added). The Jews refused to have any dealings with the Samaritans. They would not do business with them or even put their feet on Samaritan land. Jesus, however, who is the sovereign Lord of all, extended His care and love to everyone. He, yet today, welcomes all who will come to Him. We, too, must follow this example and share the gospel with all peoples.

6. John 4:24, "They that worship him *must* worship him in spirit and in truth" (emphasis added). The woman at the well was amazed to discover that Jesus knew all about her current and past life. Even more amazing was His concern for her future. He wanted her to be saved. She was, as was all her household. They yielded their hearts, souls, and devotion to the Master. We, too, must do likewise.

7. John 9:4, "I *must* work the works of him that sent me" (emphasis added). God has given each believer a spiritual gift and an obligation to use that gift in a ministry to His glory. Our earthly time is short. We must not procrastinate but, instead, be busy completing a work for the Lord.

8. John 10:16, "And other sheep I have, . . . them also I *must* bring" (emphasis added). A good shepherd will feed, protect, and nurture his flock. Jesus taught us to be shepherds. New converts are to be taught Scripture by us, be provided role models by our behavior, and be encouraged by us in all aspects of their daily walk with the Lord. It is a desirable thing to lead a person to

salvation through Christ, but the concern must not end there. Watchful shepherding will enable a new believer to grow strong spiritually.

9. John 12:34, "Christ abideth for ever: . . . The Son of man *must* be lifted up" (emphasis added). Jesus explained that the significance of His sacrificial death would be a deed by which all people would be drawn to Him. Because Christ is a member of the Godhead, He always has and always will exist. He abides forever throughout all existence, but more importantly, He is willing to abide within anyone who will accept Him as Savior.

10. John 20:9, "He *must* rise again from the dead" (emphasis added). The threescore and ten years given to men are "a vapor," but this is of no traumatic concern to those who are redeemed in Christ. Death has no victory over Christ, for He is eternal. He rose from the dead and ascended to heaven by His own will and power. One day He will return and "the dead in Christ shall rise" (1 Thess. 4:16). Because He has conquered death, we can be assured an eternal home in heaven, too.

When the Philippian jailer fell down before Paul and Silas, he asked, "Sirs, what *must* I do to be saved? And they said, Believe on the Lord Jesus Christ, and thou shalt be saved" (Acts 16:30–31, emphasis added). This is something all people *must* do to receive salvation. After that, knowing John's "Ten Must Wanted" list will serve to keep us close to the Lord and to serve Him faithfully.

THINKING MORE ABOUT CHAPTER 25

Scripture Verses to Ponder

Marvel not that I said unto thee, Ye must be born again.

—John 3:7

And as Moses lifted up the serpent in the wilderness, even so
must the Son of man be lifted up.

—John 3:14

He must increase, but I must decrease.

—John 3:30

God is a Spirit: and they that worship him must worship him
in spirit and in truth.

—John 4:24

And other sheep I have, which are not of this fold: them also
I must bring, and they shall hear my voice; and there shall be
one fold, and one shepherd.

—John 10:16

For as yet they knew not the scripture, that he must rise again
from the dead.

—John 20:9

Questions to Consider

1. The Federal Bureau of Investigation is very energetic and thorough in following through on its "Ten Most Wanted" list. How
   energetic and thorough are you in abiding by the apostle John's
   "Ten Must Wanted" list?
2. Will Rogers once joked that the only things Americans *must* do is
   die and pay taxes. If he were alive today, he might be amazed at how
   many people are able to stretch the former life span from seventy
   years to as many as eighty or ninety or more (Dr. Norman Vincent
   Peale was ninety-five when he died in December of 1993). He might
   also be amazed, in a negative way, at how many people use "loop-
   holes" to avoid paying taxes. Can you see obvious ways in which
   the *musts* of mankind are very different from the *musts* of God?

3. Each Christian is given one or more spiritual gifts from God to use in righteous ways. What are some of the things you feel you *must* do to use your talents and gifts to honor God? Make some notes.

4. How have your goals as a Christian changed during the years of your life? Were there things you felt you absolutely *must* accomplish when you were younger that now don't seem nearly as important? What lesson can you draw from this?

SUGGESTED ADDITIONAL READINGS

Cowman, Mrs. Charles E. *Streams in the Desert.* Grand Rapids: Zondervan, 1965.

Hummel, Charles E. *Tyranny of the Urgent.* Downers Grove, Ill.: InterVarsity, 1967.

Ieron, Julie-Allyson. *Praying Like Jesus.* Chicago: Moody, 2000.

Packer, J. I. *Knowing God.* Downers Grove, Ill.: InterVarsity, 1977.

Schaeffer, Francis. *How Should We Then Live?* Old Tappan, N.J.: Revell, 1976.

Tozer, Aiden W. *The Pursuit of God.* Harrisburg, Pa.: Christian Publications, 1948.

CHAPTER 26

A PENNY FOR YOUR THOUGHTS ABOUT AMERICA

Imagine, if you will, that a creature from another planet has landed on the moon and found a penny left by one of the U.S. astronauts who planted the American flag there in 1969. Just by carefully examining this penny, what would this creature be able to learn about the people of the United States?

First, he would note that we had developed an *alphabet,* for there would be writing on both sides of the coin. This would let him know that we had a system of written communication. Along this same line, he could note that we were a *multilingual* country, for the words "E Pluribus Unum" would be in Latin. That very term—"One out of many"—would indicate that our nation was composed of *many ethnic and regional peoples* from a *variety of cultures* from all over the globe.

Next, he would surmise that we were a people who understood *geometry,* since the coin would be a perfect circle, and *arithmetic,* since it would be labeled "one cent," and *history,* since the coin would be dated.

Since this was a coin, it would indicate that we had a complete *monetary system,* thus implying that we understood trade and commerce, bartering and dealing, loaning and borrowing, investing and developing.

Additionally, he would discern that we were a people who had mastered *metallurgy,* since the penny would be fashioned from mined copper and refined alloys. It would also be obvious that we had developed sophisticated *machinery,* since the coin would be stamped with perfect cuts and imprints. He could tell that we had perfected *art and design,* for the coin would be attractive, balanced, and aesthetically appealing.

By looking at the images on the coin he would be able to see that we had mastered *architecture,* for the back side of the coin would show a building with stairs, columns, walls, a roof, and a promenade. In front of the building on each side would be bushes and shrubs, indicating a mastery of *landscaping* and, thus, a knowledge of *agriculture, botany, horticulture,* and *biology.* Here, then, would be a people very knowledgeable in the *sciences.*

Observing the details of the man on the front of the coin, it could be seen that we were a people skilled at *fashion* and *tailoring,* for the man's clothes would be well-sewn. This would imply a knowledge of *textiles, patterns, and crafts.*

The coin would also reveal that these people know about *civics* and *government,* for the term "states" would indicate numerous and varied units of law, law enforcement, justice, and democracy. Furthermore, these people know about *sociology,* for the term "united" indicates people who can share, help, support, and protect one another in a spirit of cooperation. These people would be aware of the value of *historical tributes,* for there would be a man's image in the middle of a memorial building on the back of the coin. Obviously, these people know how to appreciate, remember, and laud their dedicated ancestors and great statesmen.

Having learned all this from the little penny, the stranger might wonder what the secrets were that had enabled this great nation to become so powerful and noble, so advanced and sophisticated. And the answers to these secrets would also be found there on the penny.

The first secret would be found in the nation's great motivator: "Liberty." This one word, stamped prominently on the front of the coin, would underscore this country's total dedication to freedom—complete freedom to talk, write, debate, discuss, analyze, criticize, evaluate, and have an opinion on *any* issue. Liberty, mankind's greatest love, is experienced here.

The second secret would be found in the country's national motto: "In God We Trust." This proclamation would be at the very top of the front side of the coin—above the likeness of the statesman, above the value of the coin, above the date, above *all else*. This would be the motto of a righteous people, a grateful populace, a God-honoring citizenry. More than anything else, this one clue would explain how the United States of America had become so prosperous and mighty.

> But seek ye first the kingdom of God, and his righteousness; and all these things shall be added unto you.
> —Matthew 6:33

THINKING MORE ABOUT CHAPTER 26

Scripture Verses to Ponder

> For unto us a child is born, unto us a son is given: and the government shall be upon his shoulder: and his name shall be called Wonderful, Counsellor, The mighty God, The everlasting Father, The Prince of Peace. Of the increase of his government and peace there shall be no end, upon the throne of David, and upon his kingdom, to order it, and to establish it with judgment and with justice from henceforth even for ever. The zeal of the LORD of hosts will perform this.
> —Isaiah 9:6–7

> Tell us therefore, What thinkest thou? Is it lawful to give tribute unto Caesar, or not? But Jesus perceived their wickedness,

and said, Why tempt ye me, ye hypocrites? Show me the tribute money. And they brought unto him a penny. And he saith unto them, Whose is this image and superscription? They say unto him, Caesar's. Then saith he unto them, Render therefore unto Caesar the things which are Caesar's; and unto God the things that are God's. When they heard these words, they marvelled, and left him, and went their way.

—Matthew 22:17–22

. . . them that . . . despise government. Presumptuous are they.

—2 Peter 2:10

Questions to Consider

1. Have you ever taken the time to think through issues that relate to your obligations to your country, state, and city? Are your views based on biblical teachings? Make some notes of your views on the following topics:
   • Paying taxes
   • Serving in the military
   • Voting in each election
   • Holding a political office
   • Obeying the laws of the land
2. In recent years many Christians have been put in jail because of their active protests against such things as abortion, pornography, and homosexuality. How far do you feel a Christian should be willing to go to help change laws?

SUGGESTED ADDITIONAL READINGS

Bright, Bill. *A Handbook of Concepts of Living.* San Bernardino: Here's Life, 1981.

Chambers, Oswald. *My Utmost for His Highest.* New York: Dodd, Mead and Co., 1935.

DeMoss, Arthur, and David Enlow. *How to Change Your World in Twelve Weeks.* Old Tappan, N.J.: Revell, 1969.

Goodrich, Rev. C. A. *History of the United States.* Hartford: privately published, 1824.

Lewis, C. S. *Christian Reflections.* Grand Rapids: Eerdmans, 1967.

CHAPTER 27

DROPPING A BIBLICAL
PLUMB LINE

I own some rental properties, and to save money a few years ago I repaired a patio breezeway myself rather than hire a professional carpenter to do the work.

Several timber supports were old and rotting, so I removed them and nailed in replacements. Three cross beams were evidencing dry rot, so I knocked them away and put in new ones.

The work didn't seem all that complicated. I didn't even feel the need to measure closely. I just took out the bad wood and put in the new. When I was finished, my work didn't look like a masterpiece, but I felt it was functional. Besides, two coats of fresh paint worked wonders at blending the old with the new.

I had purchased an all-weather venetian blind to attach to the open front of the breezeway. It could be lowered or raised according to the position of the sun. Try as I may, however, I couldn't figure out how to mount that blind onto the forward wall joist; so, I finally admitted my limitations and called out a carpenter. I figured, hey, it was only this one small finishing touch, so it shouldn't take him too long to fix or cost me too much, right?

When the carpenter arrived, he set up a portable workbench and unpacked his tools. He then dropped a plumb line from the roof of my adjoining house. Using this as his bearing, he measured carefully and then drilled holes into the breezeway joist. He then attached some heavy-duty brackets he had brought along and mounted the venetian blind.

When he let down the blind to test it, it was in absolute perfect alignment with the house. Unfortunately, it became very evident that my slapped-together breezeway was completely off-kilter. In fact, the carpenter was actually smiling to himself as he wrote out the bill and handed it to me.

"Nice paint job," he said with a snicker.

THE "STRAIGHT" SCOOP

I learned a good lesson that day: *A person can't see what is crooked until he has a way of determining what is straight.*

As Christians, we are constantly being measured by God to determine whether our walk and our behavior are straight. In the Old Testament, God judged His chosen people, the Jews, in that way. In Amos 7:7–8 it says that "the Lord stood upon a wall . . . with a plumbline in his hand. And the LORD said . . . Behold, I will set a plumbline in the midst of my people Israel." God measured His people against the straightness of His Word. Those who were off-kilter were brought back into line (even if it took some hammering).

In the New Testament, the apostle Paul explained to us why it is so crucial for Christians to be straight. We are the support beams and framework of Christ's church.

> So then you are no longer strangers and aliens, but you are fellow citizens with the saints, and are of God's household, having been built upon the foundation of the apostles and prophets, Christ Jesus Himself being the corner stone, in whom the whole building, being fitted together is growing

into a holy temple in the Lord; in whom *you also* are being
built together into a dwelling of God in the Spirit.
                    —Ephesians 2:19–22 NASB (emphasis added)

Ask yourself this question: Would you feel safe living in a house
that was built with wood as straight as your daily Christian walk? Would
that make you feel secure, or would you worry that the roof might fall
in at any minute? It gives you cause for thought, doesn't it?

If you ever visit my rental property with the rebuilt breezeway, you
won't be able to detect any crookedness anymore. I went back, hung a
plumb line, and brought the beams back in line with the house. It
took me several days of hard work, but I felt the result was worth the
effort. My house was in order at last.

Similarly, I regularly use the plumb line of God's Word to bring my
spiritual house back in line, too. It keeps me from the dangers of a
crooked life. I would pass that same suggestion along to you: "As for
your life, if you don't plumb it . . . you'll plummet!"

THINKING MORE ABOUT CHAPTER 27

Scripture Verses to Ponder

> Thus he shewed me: and, behold, the Lord stood upon a wall
> made by a plumbline, with a plumbline in his hand. And the
> LORD said unto me, Amos, what seest thou? And I said, A
> plumbline. Then said the Lord, Behold, I will set a plumbline
> in the midst of my people Israel: I will not again pass by them
> any more: And the high places of Isaac shall be desolate, and
> the sanctuaries of Israel shall be laid waste; and I will rise
> against the house of Jeroboam with the sword.
>   —Amos 7:7–9

For we know that if our earthly house of this tabernacle were dissolved, we have a building of God, an house not made with hands, eternal in the heavens.

—2 Corinthians 5:1

Now therefore ye are no more strangers and foreigners, but fellow-citizens with the saints, and of the household of God; And are built upon the foundation of the apostles and prophets, Jesus Christ himself being the chief corner stone; In whom all the building fitly framed together groweth unto an holy temple in the Lord: In whom ye also are builded together for an habitation of God through the Spirit.

—Ephesians 2:19–22

Questions to Consider

1. Have you ever thought about the many expressions we have that imply that a plumb line needs to be part of our lives? We tell people to "stay on the straight and narrow." We say of people who are honest that they are "straight," but people who are dishonest are "crooked." Reporters ask for the "straight scoop," and patients tell doctors, "Give it to me straight." Knowing this, when is the last time you measured yourself to see how "straight" you are? Are you straight in your talk, your business dealings, your prayers to God, your faithfulness to your spouse, and your loyalty to friends? If not, perhaps you'd better do something to "straighten yourself out."

2. In programming computers there is an acronym used by program designers: GIGO. It stands for "garbage in, garbage out." In short, if incorrect information is fed into a program, incorrect information will come out. Similarly, don't you feel that we Christians must be careful of the things we "program" into our minds? If we read the wrong kinds of books and magazines, and see the wrong kinds of movies and television shows,

won't we have more crooked information in us than straight information?

3. Many cults and pseudo-religions are perverting the Word of God today. The Bible is our plumb line to use in discerning truth. Are you using it daily to help you "keep straight"?

SUGGESTED ADDITIONAL READINGS

Cook, Bruce E., Howard Hendricks, and Stephen B. Douglas. *Ministry of Management.* San Bernardino: Here's Life, 1981.

Ferguson, David and Teresa. *Never Alone.* Wheaton: Tyndale House, 2000.

Henry, Matthew. *The Secret of Communion with God.* Westwood, N.J.: Revell, 1963.

Mitchell, Curtis. *Let's Live! Christ in Everyday Life.* Old Tappan, N.J.: Revell, 1975.

Ryken, Leland. *The Christian Imagination.* Grand Rapids: Baker, 1986.

Standford, Miles J. *The Green Letters.* Grand Rapids: Zondervan, 1982.

CHAPTER 28

THE REVEALING LIGHT

Late one rainy April night I was driving on a two-lane country road, heading home after a speaking engagement. Normally, I could have made the trip in two hours, but the poor weather conditions were slowing my progress.

Eventually the rain let up, but occasional cars passing opposite me were spraying muddy water on my windshield. My wiper blades soon became dirty, too, and instead of cleaning my windshield, they only smeared the mud in streaks.

To remedy the situation I pressed the windshield-washer button on my dashboard. No solvent squirted out, however. The reservoir under the hood was empty; I'd neglected to check it and refill it.

The wind hitting the moving car soon dried the streaked mud on my windshield, but I was able to see fairly well nevertheless. I drove along making better time.

As I came near to the city I was heading to, traffic began to pick up. I encountered more and more cars heading in the direction opposite to mine, and as each car's lights reached me, they revealed how absolutely filthy my windshield was. The oncoming lights would grow brighter and brighter, and then before me I would be able to see smears of mud, dirt, and road grime.

When the car passed and its lights no longer illuminated my car, my vehicle's window dirt would become hidden again.

As soon as I reached the city limits, I pulled into a gas station. I washed all my car windows and then refilled the reservoir of washer solvent under the hood. I also purchased an extra container of solvent and put it in my trunk, just in case I ever ran out again.

The Lord may have used that travel experience as an object lesson for me. Only a week earlier I had taught a Sunday school lesson on John 9:5, wherein Jesus said, "I am the light of the world."

I had emphasized to my students that studying the Word of God and following the path of Christ would provide "light" for our journey through life. And that was true. However, there was something more I should have added to that lesson.

Metaphorically, the light of Christ is indeed like a miner's cap. It projects a straight, clear beacon that reveals the safe path to tread. It also, however, is like a spotlight. Though we may desire to be like the muddy windshield and just travel life's road with our sins unexposed, the Bible says "the Lord . . . will bring to light the hidden things of darkness" (1 Cor. 4:5). His light shines brightly enough to reveal the stains and smears and streaks of our sins.

The apostle Paul warned the Ephesians, "All things become visible when they are exposed by the light, for everything that becomes visible is light" (Eph. 5:13 NASB). Through our consciences, through our study of God's Word, through our prayer time, the love and concern of Christ puts our sins in the spotlight. Those sins become exposed and obvious to us.

The solvent that cleanses these sins in our lives is the shed blood of Christ. Fortunately, unlike my window cleaner, it's never in short supply. Once we have accepted Christ as our Savior, we can turn to Him continually to forgive us of our sins and to cleanse us daily.

THINKING MORE ABOUT CHAPTER 28

Scripture Verses to Ponder

The LORD is my light and my salvation; whom shall I fear? the LORD is the strength of my life; of whom shall I be afraid?

—Psalm 27:1

For with thee is the fountain of life: in thy light shall we see light.

—Psalm 36:9

As long as I am in the world, I am the light of the world.

—John 9:5

Therefore judge nothing before the time, until the Lord come, who both will bring to light the hidden things of darkness, and will make manifest the counsels of the hearts: and then shall every man have praise of God.

—1 Corinthians 4:5

But all things that are reproved are made manifest by the light: for whatsoever doth make manifest is light. Wherefore he saith, Awake thou that sleepest, and arise from the dead, and Christ shall give thee light.

—Ephesians 5:13–14

Questions to Consider

1. Have you ever been in a school production or a church presentation and had a large spotlight shine directly on you? It is both wonderful and frightening, isn't it? It's wonderful because you are the center of everyone's attention and all eyes are on you. It's also frightening, however, because if you do or say anything

wrong, *everyone* will see it. This is the same situation you are in each day as you walk in God's light. You are the center of His attention; however, you are also under His constant scrutiny. How comfortable are you at being at center stage?

2. An old hymn of the faith begs, "Come to the Light, 'tis shining for thee." Have you shared this message with those around you who are still in the darkness of sin?

3. We use a lot of expressions in our language regarding light: "Then it dawned on me" . . . "If I could only see the light at the end of the tunnel" . . . "The idea came to me like a light being clicked on in my brain." We almost always refer to light as something that makes things better or reveals something to us. Jesus is the Light of the world. Isn't what He reveals to us a message that He *does* make things better?

4. Have you ever heard the expression, "It is better to light one candle than to curse the darkness"? By giving your testimony, passing out tracts, and sharing verses of Scripture, how many different places will you be able to light candles in this world?

SUGGESTED ADDITIONAL READINGS

Graham, Billy. *Storm Warning.* Dallas: Word, 1992.

MacArthur, John, Jr. *Why Believe the Bible?* Glendale, Calif.: Regal Books, 1980.

Ryrie, Charles C. *The Miracle of Our Lord.* Nashville: Nelson, 1984.

Schuller, Robert Anthony. *Getting Through the Going-Through Stage.* Nashville: Nelson, 1986.

Swindoll, Charles. *Rise and Shine: A Wake-Up Call.* Dallas: Word, 1989.

CHAPTER 29

WHOM DO YOU TRUST?

It is better to trust in the LORD than to put confidence in man.
—Psalm 118:8

When I was a little kid—back in the days of black-and-white television—there was a popular TV quiz show called *Who Do You Trust?* Teams of two contestants had to decide which of two players they trusted to answer questions in various categories of knowledge. By trusting the right person, the team could win a lot of cash and prizes. By trusting the wrong person, the team could lose all of its winnings.

The Old Testament, in 2 Samuel 11:1–27, tells a tragic version of *Who Do You Trust?* King David had been chosen of God to be a warrior king, to reclaim the land God had promised to the Jews. One year, however, David decided not to lead his men into battle. He no longer trusted God's wisdom for his life's work.

This was a grave error of judgment, for it left David in Jerusalem where he became involved in an affair with Bathsheba, the wife of Uriah, one of David's captains. When Bathsheba became pregnant, David called Uriah back from battle for a rest. He assumed that Uriah would spend the night with Bathsheba and later would think that Bathsheba's baby was Uriah's. But this was where David misjudged Uriah's character.

Uriah was a battle captain who had earned the trust of his men. He never asked them to endure anything he, himself, wasn't willing to endure. As such, even though he was no longer at the front lines while in Jerusalem, he slept outside on the ground and not inside with his wife. He remained trustworthy to his men, even when out of their sight.

Now, just as Uriah knew he was a trustworthy captain over the foot soldiers in his unit, so, too, did he assume that David was a trustworthy king over the battle captains, like himself.

But David violated that trust. He arranged a combat mishap that caused Uriah's death.

Uriah had trusted his wife and he had trusted his king, and both had betrayed him. Similarly, God had trusted David to lead the army as a general and to set an example of virtue as a king, and David had betrayed God on both counts. God sent Nathan the prophet to David to tell him that God had seen his wickedness and, as a result, the sword would never depart from his house. Strife would be a way of life from then on for David.

The story does not end there, however.

Despite his sin, David retained in his heart a deep understanding of God's love. He knew that he could ask of God, "Restoreth my soul" (Ps. 23:3).

Just as a restorer of antiques is able to scrub away the tarnish of age, David knew he could *trust* God to scrub away the tarnish of his sin. And just as a restorer of buildings rebuilds a crumbling foundation and a restorer of paintings covers darkened stains, so, too, was David able to trust God to restore the foundation of his crumbling faith and to cover the stains of his darkened transgressions.

David turned back to God, the only One he could really trust to provide forgiveness and redirection for his life. For seven days and nights David went without food. He prayed to God for mercy and care.

God forgave David of his weakness and disobedience, but He could not condone the act of David's sin with Bathsheba and the murder of Uriah. The child's life was taken. David accepted this judgment. He *trusted* God's decision.

David then set about to make amends. He married Bathsheba properly. They had a child (Solomon) whom they dedicated to God's service (2 Sam. 12:24–25). David returned to his duties as commander and led his army in a successful battle at Rabbah against the Ammonites. Once again he trusted God to direct his life.

Today, like David, we are confronted with life situations that ask us, "Whom do you trust?" We can be like David and trust our decision without concern about what God's will is for our lives. Or, through prayer and Bible study, we can seek His will in all things.

Jesus warned men not to trust in themselves (Luke 18:9). Whereas things may seem to be perfect for a time, eventually man's wisdom proves to be shallow. God's wisdom, however, is flawless.

Every day you are a contestant in life's biggest game show. The question put to you is, "Whom do you trust?" Answer correctly and a life of riches is yours (Ps. 112:1–3). Answer incorrectly and you will lose everything (Prov. 11:4). Consider carefully then: Whom *do* you trust?

THINKING MORE ABOUT CHAPTER 29

Scripture Verses to Ponder

> Though he slay me, yet will I trust in him: but I will maintain mine own ways before him. He also shall be my salvation: for an hypocrite shall not come before him.
>
> —Job 13:15–16

> What time I am afraid, I will trust in thee. In God I will praise his word, in God I have put my trust; I will not fear what flesh can do unto me.
>
> —Psalm 56:3–4

Praise ye the LORD. Blessed is the man that feareth the LORD, that delighteth greatly in his commandments. His seed shall be mighty upon the earth: the generation of the upright shall be blessed. Wealth and riches shall be in his house: and his righteousness endureth for ever.

—Psalm 112:1–3

Trust in the LORD with all thine heart; and lean not unto thine own understanding. In all thy ways acknowledge him, and he shall direct thy paths.

—Proverbs 3:5–6

Questions to Consider

1. Do you have solid trust in God? Consider each of the following people from the Bible and make a few notes about how each one had to have tremendous trust in God.
    • Abraham:

    • Sarah:

    • Isaac:

    • Noah:

    • Joseph:

    • Joshua:

    • Rahab:

    • Lydia:

2. An old hymn found in most church hymnals is titled, "Trust and Obey." In regard to the Christian faith, how are these two words inseparable?
3. How is the trust you have in Christ evident in your daily walk? Can other people sense the security you've found?

SUGGESTED ADDITIONAL READINGS

Graham, Billy. *Peace with God.* New York: Walker and Co., 1986.

———. *The Secret of Happiness.* Waco, Tex.: Word, 1988.

MacArthur, John, Jr. *Our Suffering in Christ.* Dallas: Word, 1991.

Ryrie, Charles C. *Basic Theology.* Wheaton: Victor Books, 1986.

Swindoll, Charles. *Flying Closer to the Flame.* Dallas: Word, 1993.

CHAPTER 30

THE REGENERATING
REMNANT

Throughout the Bible we can read of endless attempts that have been made to annihilate God's people and to silence the preaching of God's Word. The Egyptians tried to work the Jews to death and to murder their newborn sons, but this effort failed. The Jews survived. The Romans tried to imprison, beat, and execute the Christians, but this attempt also failed. The Christians continued to flourish.

No matter how diligently some evil force has worked to eradicate God's people, God has *always* seen to it that a remnant has survived and gone on to multiply. "Yet will I leave a remnant," the Lord has promised (Ezek. 6:8).

In today's world, with its overwhelming propensity toward ungodliness, I sometimes find myself wondering if we Christians will be able to continue to endure and survive. If I let my mind dwell on this very long, I find that I can become depressed and doubtful about it.

One autumn, however, the Lord gave me an object lesson that proved to me that His people will always survive and that, even in the worst of situations, God's remnant will remain.

Tommy, a little boy who lives down the street from me, came

knocking at my door in early September. He asked me to hurry down
to his house. He and his dad had something they wanted to show me.
It was "something amazing," he promised.

When I got there, Eric, Tommy's dad, took me to Tommy's room
and pointed to a large terrarium.

"You've written a lot of books, Doc, and I know you've studied a lot
of subjects," Eric said, "but we're looking at something here that I think
even *you* won't be able to explain."

"Oh?" I asked. "How's that?"

Eric pointed to the inside of the glass tank.

"See that snake in there? The big one? It's a female. Yesterday she
gave birth to this little-bitsy snake that's over here on the log and this
other little snake down by the saucer of water. Two babies."

I nodded. "Yes, I see them. So what?"

Little Tommy smiled broadly and interrupted. "There's no daddy.
She had babies without there being a daddy snake."

I looked puzzled. I turned to Eric.

"He's right," said Eric. "We bought this snake thirty-two months
ago at a pet store. She's been in this tank alone that whole time, except
for the grasshoppers and minnows we feed her. No other snakes have
been near her. Yet, last night she gave birth to two baby snakes. Now,
how do you explain *that?*"

"Was she pregnant when you got her?" I asked.

"Nope," said Eric. "I even called the pet store owner to make sure.
He said these snakes mate in the spring and give birth four months
later in autumn. So, she couldn't have been pregnant when we bought
her nearly three years ago."

"Then this is impossible," I said, bewildered.

Tommy laughed. "Try telling that to the two baby snakes!"

My curiosity was piqued. I wrote down a precise description of the
snake, as well as details of its years as Tommy's pet. That afternoon I
phoned Dr. Jennifer Mains, a veterinarian who supervises the
serpentarium at our state's largest zoo. I gave her the details and asked
if she had any logical explanation.

"Ah, yes," said Dr. Mains, "what you've described is a member of the *reptilia* family known as the 'ribbon snake.' It's truly one of nature's great wonders. In the spring, the female 'accepts' sperm from the male snake. However, the female has the ability to keep the sperm alive inside of her *yet separated* from her eggs for up to three years. Only when she feels secure in her surroundings and convinced that there will be enough food and water to support her young will she let the sperm fertilize her eggs.

"Once her eggs are fertilized, they go through a four-month gestation period and then are born alive—not in eggs the way most other snakes are born. Anywhere from two to six babies will be born at one time. The newborn snakes are covered with a membrane, which they break free of themselves by crawling on the ground. They then begin immediately to search for food."

"That's incredible," I said, truly amazed.

"I agree," said Dr. Mains. "The ribbon snake can live ten or twelve years, and can grow as long as four feet and become as thick as a man's thumb. They make great pets because they aren't poisonous and, thus, have no fangs. They just have a small row of tiny teeth used to position their prey, which they swallow whole. Their strong stomach acids can digest everything except bones and fur. They are true survivors.

"In fact," she continued, "back during World War II, a small island needed for a landing strip was cleared of all snakes except for *one* ribbon snake, which an airman kept in a jar as his pet. Three years later, when the military pulled out, the airman released that one female snake into the underbrush. He felt it couldn't harm anything since she had no one to mate with. Within two years the island was overrun with ribbon snakes. She had carried the sperm in her those three years in the jar."

"So, Tommy's snake must have been holding sperm in it when it was purchased," I speculated, "but it took the snake a couple of years in the new terrarium to become convinced it was a safe place to give birth to her young?"

"Exactly," said Dr. Mains. "And if one of the newborns is a male, then more snakes will be on the way very soon. You'd better warn Tommy about that." She chuckled as she added this last bit of information.

After hanging up the phone, it occurred to me that if God could so miraculously devise a survival plan that allowed a lowly snake to protect itself from extinction, how much greater must His plan be for the endurance and continuance of His own children.

The Bible says, "The Lord is faithful, and He will strengthen and protect you from the evil one" (2 Thess. 3:3 NASB). Thousands of years of history have proven this to be true. While other peoples and nations have disappeared from the face of the earth, God's children have remained. Though sometimes reduced to a remnant, they have always come back strong.

During pioneer times in America, packaged yeast was hard to obtain. As such, women made their own. They would pinch off a small portion of their bread dough whenever they were baking. They'd set this piece of raw dough aside. Within two days it would ferment, or "go sour," and become laden with entrapped yeast organisms. A week later this small piece of sour dough would be so potent, it could be mixed with a huge bowl of water and flour to create several loaves of new bread. In the process, however, the cook would pinch off a small portion of the new dough and let it go sour so that the procedure could continue over and over.

Just as a meager pinch of bread dough could "give rise" to many loaves, so, too, can a small remnant of God's faithful people regenerate a large, faithful body of believers.

A remnant is small . . . but it is all that is needed.

THINKING MORE ABOUT CHAPTER 30

Scripture Verses to Ponder

> In all your dwelling places the cities shall be laid waste, and the high places shall be desolate; that your altars may be laid waste and made desolate, and your idols may be broken and cease, and your images may be cut down, and your works may be abolished. And the slain shall fall in the midst of you,

and ye shall know that I am LORD. Yet will I leave a remnant, that ye may have some that shall escape the sword among the nations, when ye shall be scattered through the countries.

—Ezekiel 6:6–8

Finally, brethren, pray for us, that the word of the Lord may have free course, and be glorified, even as it is with you: And that we may be delivered from unreasonable and wicked men: for all men have not faith. But the Lord is faithful, who shall stablish you, and keep you from evil. And we have confidence in the Lord touching you, that ye both do and will do the things which we command you.

—2 Thessalonians 3:1–4

Questions to Consider

1. Have you ever stopped to think of how many dozens of nations and peoples (Zorathites, Ziphims, Tarpelites, Perizzites, Philistines, Canaanites, etc.) mentioned in the Bible have completely disappeared from the face of the earth because they showed no love and respect for God? What lesson can be drawn from this in light of modern history, such as the defeat of Saddam Hussein in "Desert Storm" (1991) and the end of the Cold War at the Yeltsin-Bush Peace Conference (1992)? Do we have evidence that God is still judging nations that turn from Him?

2. After the Great Flood, only Noah and his extended family were left to replenish the earth; nevertheless, today there are billions of people on the globe. What lessons can we draw from this as to God's ability both to reduce and expand the world's population?

3. When Jesus left this earth, He left a remnant of disciples. From them grew the great Christian movement we have in the world today. Can you think of other examples in the Bible in which a remnant was used to found a great work of God?

4. How does God use nature to give examples of a remnant being able to restore growth? [Hints: One seed pod can produce fifty flowers. One acorn can grow an eighty-five-foot tree.]
5. Remnants exist everywhere. If you were the leader of a prayer group and you had to move, couldn't you begin again in a new neighborhood? Try to see your growth potential for the Lord.

SUGGESTED ADDITIONAL READINGS

Graham, Billy. *Hope for the Troubled Heart.* Dallas: Word, 1991.
MacArthur, John, Jr. *The Family.* Chicago: Moody, 1982.
Ryrie, Charles C. *The Holy Spirit.* Chicago: Moody, 1965.
Swindoll, Charles. *Laugh Again.* Dallas: Word, 1992.
———. *Simple Faith.* Dallas: Word, 1991.

CHAPTER 31

THE X FACTOR IN CHRISTMAS

One December evening back when my son was still in high school, I was helping him with his algebra homework. Each problem was presented with a variety of multiples on the left and right sides of an equal (=) sign. In each problem the challenge was to figure out what the X factor was (i.e., the unknown quantity). Once X was solved, it could be multiplied by the given numbers and both sides of the equation would balance.

After an hour of working calculations, we had finally finished the assignment. We decided to drive downtown to do some Christmas shopping. As we drove past the various shopping malls, we saw signs reading "Xmas Trees for Sale" and "Mail Early for Xmas" and "Xmas Gift Wrapping Sold Here."

I nodded at all the signs. "Even for Christmas it seems that X is the unknown factor," I said to my son. "Everybody wants to find 'Peace on Earth' and 'Good Will Toward Men,' but they can't solve the problems of the world until they discover that the unknown factor is Christ."

"They need a formula," suggested my son, Nathan, "or a reference equation. You know: something like 'X equals N squared' or 'X equals 15 plus 2 Y.' There has to be a common number or base factor."

I pondered that awhile, then said, "I think the New Testament is filled with reference equations that explain what X is equal to."

"Oh?" asked Nathan. "Like what?"

"Well," I began, "how about 'X equals 70 times 7' in regard to forgiveness? Or how about 'X equals 1,000' when it comes to the number of hills on which God owns cattle? Or how about 'X equals 99 plus one' when it comes to rescuing the lost sinner?"

My son smiled, then said, "Sure. Or X could also equal two, in regard to Christ's second coming . . . or three, in that the Father, Son, and Holy Spirit are one God."

I added, "Or X could equal 500 plus 50 when it comes to forgiving all debtors" (Luke 7:41).

"Or X could equal 70 in regard to sending out hosts of missionaries," continued Nathan (Luke 10:1).

I parked the car in front of a department store.

"That's a pretty good start," I said. "We could probably make a sizable list with all sorts of mathematical variables, but in each instance the equation would only be balanced if we substituted Jesus for the unknown factor. Whatever is missing, whatever is needed . . ."

". . . Jesus leads to the solution," said Nathan.

"Right," I agreed. "You're pretty sharp."

My son tapped the side of his forehead with his index finger and replied, "Not sharp . . . just X-cellent!"

THINKING MORE ABOUT CHAPTER 31

Scripture Verses to Ponder

> And in the sixth month the angel Gabriel was sent from God unto a city of Galilee, named Nazareth, To a virgin espoused to a man whose name was Joseph, of the house of David; and the virgin's name was Mary. And the angel came in unto her,

and said, Hail, thou that art highly favoured, the Lord is with thee: blessed art thou among women. And when she saw him, she was troubled at his saying, and cast in her mind what manner of salutation this should be. And the angel said unto her, Fear not, Mary: for thou hast found favour with God. And, behold, thou shalt conceive in thy womb, and bring forth a son, and shalt call his name Jesus. He shall be great, and shall be called the Son of the Highest: and the Lord God shall give unto him the throne of his father David: And he shall reign over the house of Jacob for ever; and of his kingdom there shall be no end.

—Luke 1:26–33

For unto us a child is born, unto us a son is given: and the government shall be upon his shoulder: and his name shall be called Wonderful, Counsellor, The mighty God, The everlasting Father, The Prince of Peace. Of the increase of his government and peace there shall be no end, upon the throne of David, and upon his kingdom, to order it, and to establish it with judgment and with justice from henceforth even for ever. The zeal of the LORD of hosts will perform this.

—Isaiah 9:6–7

Questions to Consider

1. In Dickens' famous novel *A Christmas Carol*, it was said that old Ebeneezer Scrooge learned to carry Christmas in his heart all year round. What aspects of Christmas do you think you do a good job of carrying in your heart all year long? What are some aspects of the spirit of Christmas that you are guilty of forgetting as the year moves on? Are there ways you might do a better job of maintaining the positive aspects of Christmas all twelve months?

2. In this chapter we saw how the world wants to put an *X* through

the name of Christ. Can you think of ways this is done during other holidays or other events during the year? Is there something you could do to keep Christ from being crossed out of people's lives?

3. Isn't it a shame that we only sing Christmas carols in December? What's wrong with having "Joy to the World" in March? Don't the herald angels sing Christ's praises in April, too? Can't we focus on the event of that little town in Bethlehem in July or September? Of course, the answer to each of these questions is, "Yes!" So, play some Christmas music today. It'll help you carry the message of Christmas throughout the year.

4. The Bible is filled with mathematical X factors that show the increase of God's blessings to us. This chapter listed several good examples, but can you find others?

SUGGESTED ADDITIONAL READINGS

Fuller, Cheri. *Creating Christmas Memories.* Tulsa: Honor Books, 1991.

Heller, David. *The Best Christmas Presents Are Wrapped in Heaven.* New York: Villard Books, 1993.

Hensley, Dennis. *Surprises and Miracles of the Season: Devotions for Christmas and New Year's.* Kansas City: Beacon Hill Press, 2002.

MacArthur, John. *God with Us: The Miracle of Christmas.* Grand Rapids: Zondervan, 1989.

McCullough, Bonnie. *An Old-Fashioned Christmas.* Des Moines: Meredith Books, 1992.

Shea, John. *Starlight: Beholding the Christmas Miracle All Year Long.* New York: Crossroad Books, 1993.

Ten Boom, Corrie. *Christmas Memories.* Old Tappan, N.J.: Revell, 1989.

ABOUT THE AUTHOR

Dr. Dennis E. Hensley is the author of six novels and thirty-four nonfiction books, including *Money Wise* (Harvest House), *The Jesus Effect* (Pacific Press), *How to Write What You Love and Make a Living at It* (Random House), *How to Stop Living for the Applause* (Servant Publishers), *Uncommon Sense* (Bobbs-Merrill), and *Millennium Approaches* (Avon). He is the author of the four books/four audiotapes "Success in Christian Living" series published by Warner Press.

Dr. Hensley holds four university degrees in communication skills, including a Ph.D. in literature and linguistics from Ball State University, where he was named "Distinguished Doctoral Graduate in English." In 1990 he received the "Excellence in Teaching Award" from Indiana University. In 1993 he was the recipient of the "Dorothy Hamilton Writing Award" given in recognition of his careers as a journalist and a writing instructor. In 1994 he was awarded a "Bicentennial Gold Medallion" by the City of Fort Wayne, for outstanding achievement as an author. From 2001 to 2002 he served as Distinguished Visiting Professor of English and Journalism at the graduate communications school of Regent University.

Dr. Hensley has published more than three thousand freelance articles in such periodicals as *Confident Living*, *The Baptist Bulletin*,

Evangel, Light and Life, Conquest, The War Cry, Young Salvationist, Standard, The Lookout, Contact, Messenger, The Christian Reader, Purpose, Young Ambassador, Vital Christianity, Signs of the Times, Stereo, Downbeat, Guitar Player, ABA Journal: The Lawyer's Magazine, Success! The Writer, Reader's Digest, People, Modern Bride, Progressions, The Detroit Free Press, The Indianapolis Star, and *The Cincinnati Enquirer.* He was a correspondent for *Writer's Digest* for twenty-two years, and has written more than seventy-five major features for that magazine. He is a professor of English at the Fort Wayne campus of Taylor University, where he directs the professional writing major. He also sits on the Editorial Board of the Christian Writers Guild.

Dr. Hensley has served numerous times as a judge for the annual Evangelical Press Association Awards and the Christy Fiction Awards. Each year he is a keynote speaker and workshop leader at writers' conferences nationwide.

Active in his local church as a deacon and Sunday school teacher, Dr. Hensley also served ten years as the school board chairman of a Christian elementary school. He and his wife, Rose, have a son, Nathan, and a daughter, Jeanette.